LOST KEY'S
TO
THE KINGDOM

Over Three Decades of
Experience in One Book

To Vern & Jean,
precious servants of our
Lord! May God continue
to bless & prosper you! Stan

By Stan Johnson

ISBN 0-9768212-0-6

First Printing

DEDICATION

To The Lord Jesus Christ, for the revelation He gave me and for making it possible to share it in this book.

To Betty, my loving wife and dedicated co-laborer in our ministry. For her support and hours of prayer.

To my children who are willing to help me any way they can. Especially to my son Jay, for his time and help on the book cover and my good friend Tom Waddington for the design.

To all partners and friends who helped in their support, prayers and encouragement.

TABLE OF CONTENTS

Foreword

Stan Johnson has indeed found a principal in God's word that has been lost to the body of Christ for many years. It really did not come from deep study in the word, but by a revelation from God during a deliverance service at Grace Tabernacle Church in Loris, S.C. many years ago. How do I know this? I was there. On that night there were several ministry teams at work in different areas of our church. My brother Stan happened to be ministering near the alter to a young man who was prostate on the floor by our Grand Piano. He was really causing a commotion. He became so violent with his feet that he was kicking the side of our Grand Piano. The young man had reached the point that he was not only destructive to property but was dangerous to people as well. Suddenly my brother Stan received a word from God that said "according to Matt 18:18 bind his feet." As Stan obeyed, to everyone's utter amazement, the mans feet were bound to the floor and he could not move them. My brother continued the deliverance and finished delivering the boy from the violent demons. The boy was unable to move his feet during the entire episode which must have lasted an hour or more. When the deliverance was complete, and the boy was set free, Stan gave the command "I loose your feet according to Matt 18:18 in Jesus name" and instantly he was able to move his feet again.

After I had seen this, the same night I had a similar experience. While several of us were ministering to a teenage girl who had been involved in Witchcraft, she also became violent. Using her arms and hands, she began to attack those of us who were ministering to her. She would scratch at our faces trying to get to our eyes. She had the strength of several men and was hard to handle. Several of us had her hands pinned to the floor behind her head. After seeing how God had used my brother earlier in the evening, faith rose up within me and I said to the woman, "According to Matt 18:18 I bind your hands to the floor" and we let go. To mine and everyone's amazement, her hands were bound to the floor and as much as she tried, she could not get them free.

To hear about this happening somewhere else might make it hard to believe. I was there; I saw it happen and did it myself. We should be doing what Jesus told us to do and not be afraid of the violent reactions of the enemy. Jesus said *behold, I give unto you power to tread on serpents and scorpions, and over all the power of the enemy: and nothing shall by any means hurt you* (Luke 10:19).

After the seven sons' of Sceva had their encounter with a violent demon possessed man they probably retired from their deliverance ministry, but for us, a lost key has been found and we should go forth into ministry with all the keys and not just one or two. This book by Stan Johnson is not just enlightening and faith building, but is a necessary weapon in our arsenal. Every serious minded believer should read this book and have it in their library.

Pastor Owen Johnson
Loris, SC

ENDORSEMENTS

It is about time! After almost 30 years in the ministry Stan Johnson has given to the Church some needed insight and wisdom on the principles of binding and loosing. Early in my ministry [in the early 70's] the Lord showed me and gave to me, through a deliverance experience of a pastor bound with a spirit of perversion, a little insight into the ministry of binding and loosing. After many days of trying to set the captives free the Lord gave me and two other pastors a vision of this poor pastor's hands and feet being bound with chains. He then showed us how to set this pastor free through the principles of binding and loosing. In the mid 80's I met Stan Johnson and sat under his anointed teachings on deliverance and especially on binding and loosing; they impacted my life and countless others, as the years have gone by many have been set free by the Holy Spirit as these principles have been applied over and over again. Stan, thank you! This book is long over due.

Dr. Robert W. Roach, D.Min.
PhD. President Freedom Seminary
PORT ST. LUCIE, FL.

It has been my privilege to know Stan and Betty Johnson for more than 20 years. I have learned much through their anointed teaching and have witnessed personally, numerous healings, miracles, and deliverances among the body of Christ, following their ministry. I myself have been on numerous occasions powerfully ministered to by the Holy Spirit working through them.

I am very thankful for the manner which Stan and Betty have laid down their lives for the gospel and their un-wavering commitment in helping those in needs. I have often observed their unfeigned compassion for the sick and afflicted, as well as for the lost, bound, and oppressed. Whether in large church services, or the humblest home gatherings, they pour out themselves as drink offerings, upon the dry, parched dust of a suffering humanity.

Our Lord Jesus has gifted our dear brother and sister with keen insight and revelation as to how best to help those in need of divine intervention. Certain "key's" have been entrusted to them, which when properly taught and understood, have the potential to open the prison gates (spiritually speaking) to multitudes especially effective is the understanding of "binding & loosing," which Stan has taught and practiced in churches and fellowships both at home and abroad. Another remarkable teaching which has ushered many out of the dark shadows of bondage to sin and habit is, "The 12 Gates of the City." With gratitude, I wish Stan and Betty many fruitful years of ministry and our Lord's blessings on this book.

Michael O'Connor- Pastor
New Haven, CT

The Revelation of Binding & Loosing

God's voice spoke to me, "Bind his feet according to Matt 8:18," as I ministered deliverance to a teenager in my brother's church. He was lying on the platform, kicking the piano violently, and screaming "I hate my daddy." Over and over he kicked and screamed the hatred he felt for his father. God raised His voice and very clearly said to me, "Bind his feet according to Matthew 18:18."

I have ministered to many people before that manifested their anger and hatred toward someone and I would gently restrain them by holding their feet and hands to keep them from injuring themselves or someone present; however I never had bound a "**person**" using the binding and loosing principal. "**Verily I say unto you, whatsoever ye shall bind on earth shall be bound in heaven: and whatsoever ye shall loose on earth shall be loosed in heaven.**"

Not understanding how I could bind someone's feet using that scripture, I softly said "I bind your feet according to Matt 18:18 in Jesus' name." Instantly his feet came together as though an invisible rope had been wrapped around his ankles and secured to the floor. I was shocked to see this binding principal work, restraining this person from his violent behavior.

The rage and violence started using his hands as he lay on his stomach, repeatedly hitting the floor, screaming, "I hate my daddy." Over and over he pounded the floor as if he was beating his daddy and God said, "Bind his hands the same way." This time I spoke with more confidence saying, "I bind your hands in Jesus' name." Instantly both hands went palms down as though his hands had been nailed to the floor. Other parts of his body moved violently as he layed there thrashing on the floor. It seemed everything was free to move except his hands and feet. God then said," **now you have the "strong" man bound so spoil his house by taking the goods out." (Spirits & bondages are the goods)!** The goods were the spirits in him that were manifesting their personalities of hatred, anger, rage, violence, destruction, and many other bondages that had troubled this young man. One by one the Holy Spirit told me what to cast out and the boy was held hands and feet until all the spirits had been removed and he was set free.

The Greek word to bind is Deo which means to bind, fasten, or tie with any sort of binding. I had just seen all of this manifested in the young man!
In the Nelsons Complete Study Bible, binding refers to the things not permitted while loosing refers to that which is permitted. In Matt 16:19 the tenses imply that what is loosed or bound on earth have been determined already in heaven. We know that it has already been determined in heaven that God wants people to go free from all the oppression of the devil! He has made a way, with the keys, to tie up the person (strong man) if needed to set him free.

The Greek word for loose is Luo and means to loosen, unbind, release, or untie. **We know that this has already been determined in heaven because Jesus became sin for us and bore our sicknesses, carried our infirmities, and took stripes so that we could be healed! He has paid the price for us and wants to forgive all our iniquities, and heal all of our diseases!**

Most of his trouble had come through a root of bitterness that had gained entrance in him through his daddy not using wisdom in correcting and raising him as a child. Many people today need to be delivered from evil spirits as a result of being abused physically, emotionally, sexually, and by other means. God warns us concerning the dangers of allowing a root of bitterness to spring up in us. The root of bitterness is a spiritual root made up of many spirits! **Remember spirits need to be cast out!**

It says in Heb 12:15, "looking carefully lest anyone fall short of the grace of God; lest any root of bitterness springing up trouble you, and thereby many be defiled."
Many people today have trouble with a root of bitterness tormenting them and are in return defiling many people with the

bitterness that speaks through their mouth. James says that the tongue is an unruly evil and is full of deadly poison. Deadly poison is used to execute people on death row. If we do not forgive people who have offended us, the torment will remain and the root of bitterness will end up eating us alive (poisoning us). The scriptures tell us that life and death are in the power of the tongue and a man is satisfied by the fruit of it. What we say is not only affecting people that hear us but also ourselves! It is for our own well being that we forgive those who did us wrong as well as ourselves!

The Strong Man Bound

Matt12:29 had just manifested before my eyes.
"Or how can one enter a strong man's house and plunder his goods, unless he first binds the strong man? And then he will plunder his house." Notice Jesus did not say to bind Satan, demons, angels, principalities, or powers, but clearly said man. God's people seem to be binding everything but the **man**. We work in the natural realm and Jesus said his Father worked in the spiritual or heavenly realm. God holds them while we cast out the spirits, setting them free.

There is much confusion concerning binding the strong man before plundering his house.

In the following deliverance of the blind and dumb boy, Jesus was accused of using Beelzebub's power to cast out spirits. Jesus was binding the strong man here and stated that for him to have evil power to cast out spirits, he would have to have an evil power within him. Jesus made the statement in John 14:30, *"I will no longer talk much with you, for the ruler of this world is coming, and he has nothing in me. Jesus did not have any evil in him that could be used to cast out the blind and dumb spirit."*

In Matt 12:25-26 25 *"But Jesus knew their thoughts, and said*

12

to them: Every kingdom divided against itself is brought to desolation, and every city or house divided against itself will not stand. ²⁶If Satan casts out Satan, he is divided against himself. How then will his kingdom stand?"

Here Jesus was telling them that Satan was not casting out Satan and if he was, his kingdom would not stand. Jesus said their children were casting out spirits using his name, which is the proper way, and they would end up being their judge.
^{22"}Then one was brought to Him who was demon-possessed, blind and mute; and He healed him, so that the blind and mute man both spoke and saw. ²³And all the multitudes were amazed and said, "Could this be the Son of David?" ²⁴Now when the Pharisees heard it they said, "This fellow does not cast out demons except by Beelzebub, the ruler of the demons."
²⁵But Jesus knew their thoughts, and said to them: "Every kingdom divided against itself is brought to desolation divided against himself. How then will his kingdom stand? ²⁷And if I cast out demons by Beelzebub, by whom do your sons cast them out? Therefore they shall be your judges. ²⁸But if I cast out demons by the Spirit of God, surely the kingdom of God has come upon you. ²⁹Or how can one enter a strong man's house and plunder his goods, unless he first binds the strong man? And then he will plunder his house. ³⁰He who is not with me is against me, and he who does not gather with me scatters abroad."(Matt:12:22-32) and every city or house divided against itself will not stand.*

The Unpardonable Sin

^{31"}And so I tell you, every sin and blasphemy will be forgiven men, but the blasphemy against the Holy Spirit will not be forgiven, either in this age or in the age to come".

For Satan to have something evil in Jesus he would have had to bind (entangle) him in sin, and according to Galatians corruption (Satan's power) would have been sowed to Jesus' flesh which would have produced the works of the flesh; one of which is witchcraft. Jesus was not using witchcraft to cast out devils but the Holy Spirit (finger of God).

People learning how to minister deliverance today are very confused about binding the strong man. Some say the strong man is Satan. Some say angels, others say, things like anger, hate, rejection, depression, lust, etc.

Jesus clearly said to bind the strong "MAN!" Jesus knew the difference between a man and all the other things we are trying to bind. The Apostle Paul said if we are not careful we will be fighting Satan and his kingdom by beating the air with our fist! He must be fought with truth!

A Tree Known by Its Fruit

"Either make the tree good and its fruit good, or else make the tree bad and its fruit bad; for a tree is known by its fruit". To be delivered from a root of bitterness we must ask ourselves what initially established it within us. Someone or some situation happened at some point in our life, and it is imperative that we forgive the person that caused it. The spirits will not leave unless you forgive and release the person for what they did to you.

This principal is explained by Jesus himself in Mark 11:25-*26* *"And whenever you stand praying, if you have anything against anyone, forgive him, that your Father in heaven may also forgive you your trespasses. *26*But if you do not forgive neither will your Father in heaven forgive your trespasses."* We are turned over to demons of torment until we forgive.

Many people are having severe emotional problems and some nervous breakdowns because they are unwilling to forgive the people who have offended or abused them. We must walk in forgiveness if we want the peace of God to rule and reign in our life.

You Don't Have To Forgive God

Do not fall into the trap of feeling you have to forgive God. God is perfect in all His ways and has never made a mistake or committed a sin. All of His judgments and actions are perfect. God once said that He gets blamed for many things He did not do. We must remember that Satan has come to steal, kill, and destroy. This is the law of sin and death at work in the world

- God is not causing it but the devil! It is bad doctrine to say that God allows everything that happens in our lives and the lives of others.

Because of this teaching, people get mad at God for the terrible things that have happened to them, and thus, at times feel like they have to forgive God for the evil things that He has allowed. When it comes to our relationship with God we must be willing to say, "Though He slay me, yet will I trust Him."

Another good example of this is found in Matt. 18:21-35:

[21]"Then Peter came to Him and said, "Lord, how often shall my brother sin against me, and I forgive him? Up to seven times?" [22]Jesus said to him, "I do not say to you, up to seven times, but up to seventy times seven. [23]Therefore the kingdom of heaven is like a certain king who wanted to settle accounts with his servants. [24]And when he had begun to settle accounts, one was brought to him who owed him ten thousand talents. [25]But as he was not able to pay, his master commanded that he be sold, with his wife and children and that the entire payment be made. [26]The servant therefore fell down before him, saying, "Master, have patience with me, and I will pay you all.' [27]Then the master of that servant was moved with compassion, released him, and forgave him the debt. [28]"But that servant went out and found one of his fellow servants who owed him a hundred denarii; and he laid hands on him and took him by the throat, saying, "Pay me what you owe!' [29]So his fellow servant fell down at his feet and begged him, saying, "Have patience with me, and I will pay you all. [30]And he would not, but went and threw him into prison till he should pay the debt. [31]So when his fellow servants saw what had been done, they were very grieved, and came and told their master all that had been done. [32]Then his master, after he had called him, said to him, "You wicked servant! I forgave you all that debt because you begged me. [33]Should you not also have had compassion on your fellow servant, just as I had pity on you?' [34]And his master was angry, and delivered him to the torturers (evil spirits) until he should pay all that was due to him. [35]"So My heavenly Father also will do to you if each of you, from his heart, does not forgive his brother his trespasses."

This illustration Jesus used is very descriptive of what He expects of people that have received his forgiveness and mercy, but are not willing to forgive or show mercy to others. While we were yet sinners, he died for us that we could be forgiven and released from the burden and torment of sin. Jesus expects us to forgive and show mercy to others as we would want Him to do for us. The torturers referred to in verse 34 are the causes of the trouble in our flesh and emotions. Many sicknesses, diseases, and infirmities are the result of un-forgiveness. Some of these things must be cast out in order to set the captives free!

Many people today in mental hospitals are bound up with the root of bitterness and are thus in a mental prison with cruel and unrelenting torment holding them in captivity. Wouldn't it be tragic for people in these conditions to be blaming God for allowing these things to happen to them?

Satan causes it and then laughs when the people blame God for it! No wonder he is called the deceiver! We are commanded by the Lord Jesus Christ in the great commission to preach deliverance to the captives and tell them to forgive, so they can be released from the prison of torment! God says my people perish for lack of knowledge! In the scriptures we are told to be strong in the Lord and in the power of His might. We are in a spiritual war and to be effective and survive we must know how to properly wage war against our enemy, the kingdom of darkness.

We are supposed to be doing the same works Jesus did and set people free from their bondages and torments. God wants his people free!

A missionary and his wife came to our home several years ago to be delivered from evil spirits that manifested and embarrassed them on the mission field. He had a problem with anger and rage that was constantly troubling him and his wife. As he paced the floor he said "Stan Johnson, if you get these things stirred up in me I will tear your house up." This was a strong and husky man weighing well over 200 lbs. God said for us to be wise as serpents and harmless as doves. This event made me realize I had to be better prepared to deal with this and other situations without being afraid. I was very concerned and waited for God to give me his wisdom - He said in his word that he would give his wisdom liberally to everyone that would ask. Look at the following person Jesus ran into: He was exceedingly fierce *"When He had come to the other side, to the country of the Gergesenes, there met Him two demon-possessed men, coming out of the tombs, exceedingly fierce, so that no one could pass that way."* We will be facing many violent and aggressive people in the future and we need to be ready and know how to handle each situation. God said, "Tell him to go fast and pray, humbling himself, and then I will set him free." Needless to say, I needed for God to show me something that would assure me to never hesitate or be afraid confronting any type of situation in the future. Within 24 hours God showed me the revelation of effectively using Matt 18:18; whatever you bind and loose on earth, shall be bound and loosed in heaven! This kingdom is described in Ephesians 6:12, for we do not wrestle against flesh and blood, but against principalities, against powers, against the rulers of the darkness of this age, against spiritual hosts of wickedness in the heavenly places. This kingdom is ruled and controlled by Satan, the Prince and power of the air. He was kicked out of heaven along with 1/3 of the angels that followed him in rebelling against God. Satan and his kingdom have one purpose which is to steal, kill, and destroy. His kingdom is a spiritual kingdom that is used to work through human flesh to do his evil and destructive deeds in the earth. This kingdom of darkness is evident as we see it working in people today! The works or actions of the flesh are listed in Gal 5:19 [19]Now the works of the flesh are evident, which are: adultery, fornication, uncleanness, lewdness, [20]idolatry, sorcery, hatred, contentions, jealousies, outbursts of wrath, selfish ambitions, dissensions, heresies, [21]envy, murders, drunkenness, revelries, and the like; of which I tell you beforehand, just as I also told you in time past, that those who practice such things will not inherit the kingdom of God. Jesus came to save us from the **works of the devil** which are the **works of the flesh.** The devil and his corruption are what we wrestle against. Paul said in Rom 6:16 [16]Do you not know that to whom you present yourselves slaves to obey; you are that one's slaves whom you obey, whether of sin leading to death, or of obedience leading to righteousness? **Satan received his authority to rule in the lives of humanity when Adam and Eve were disobedient, eating of the forbidden fruit in the garden planted by God. They sowed and allowed the law of sin and death to enter their flesh and thus our real enemies are working inside of and through us to cause the works of the flesh in the lives of people! Jesus said the kingdom of God suffers violence and the violent take it by force. Jesus also said the kingdom of God is within us... Our real battles are taking place inside of us!**

The things we wrestle against - the lust of the eyes, the lust of the flesh, and the pride of life, gained entrance into human flesh through Adam and Eve's transgressions. These three strongholds cause us to sow other things to our flesh called corruption. Gal 6:8 *"For he that soweth to his flesh shall of the flesh reap spiritual corruption,* which is spirit in nature, and thus can be cast out according to Jesus commandments "In my name they shall cast out spirits."Anger, rage, violence, destruction, and vengeance are only some of the "spirits" of corruption. God's people have sown much corruption to their flesh over the years and God said in Gal 6:8 that if we do not believe that we can sow and have corruption in our flesh as Christians, we are deceived! Many of God's people are deceived, including many ministers of the gospel and sometimes even entire denominations. We need to confess our sins and be forgiven and cleansed by the blood of Jesus Christ that was shed for us at Calvary. The need for deliverance is to have the corruption removed that came in through our sins or transgressions. This need is described in 2nd Cor 7:1 *" [1] Therefore, having these promises, beloved, let us cleanse ourselves from all filthiness of the **flesh and spirit,** perfecting holiness in the fear of God."* The Lord is saying this to born again Christians! God explained to Daniel the prophet this principal concerning the end of time which I believe we are now living in. *"And he said "Go your way, Daniel, for the words are closed up and sealed till the time of the end. [10]Many shall be purified, made white, and refined, but the wicked shall do wickedly; and none of the wicked shall understand, but the wise shall understand".* (Daniel 12:9-10).

There are many unwise Christians today that do not understand this principal and thus are confused as to why they do not have more victory in their walk with the Lord. Paul said we **serve** the corruption we have yielded to which is holding us in bondage and working to keep us out of the perfect will of God. Many people today have not received their healing and wonder why the manifestation of their healing has not come. Some have been anointed with oil, had hands laid on them, and confessed that they were healed by Jesus stripes, but their healing has not manifested. If they need to have the spirits cast out in order for their healing to manifest, they need to apply the following principal to receive their healing…Luke 8:2 *"and certain women, who had been healed of evil spirits and infirmities, Mary called Mag-da-le-ne, out of who went seven devil."* She would not have been healed if Jesus had not dealt with the evil spirits. Many Christians today do not receive their healing because evil spirits are not being dealt with and cast out when needed. Many people today make fun of the deliverance ministers by making statements like: "they see a demon behind every bush." If they knew the truth there are many cases where there are several behind every bush, but many of God's people do not know how to recognize them and thus they wonder why more people are not healed and have more victory in their lives

Who Was Holding the Boy Down?

I like to understand how things happen and what makes them work so I asked God to show me in his word who was holding the boy down when I bound his hands and feet. The following is where the Lord took me in his word.

All wisdom and knowledge can be found in the word of God. The Apostle Paul said to prove all things and to hold fast to that which is good. We must in these days, go to the scriptures to prove out what we are going to believe and act on. We are not to be repeaters of what we have been taught until we have proved all things and hold fast and teach that which has been proven to be good. Our very lives and the lives of many others are at stake! God led me to *Heb 1:13 "…To which of the angels has He ever said: "Sit at My right hand, till I make your enemies your footstool"?* ^{14}*Are they not all ministering spirits sent forth to minister for those who will inherit salvation?"* I have inherited salvation by believing and trusting in Jesus Christ and calling on his name, therefore the angels will assist me as I minister.

In Revelation 22:8-9 *"Now I, John, saw and heard these things. And when I heard and saw, I fell down to worship before the feet of the angel who showed me these things.* ^{9}*Then he said to me, See that you do not do that. For I am your fellow servant, and of your brethren the prophets, and of those who keep the words of this book. Worship God."*

We know by faith that angels are camped round about us to deliver us in times of trouble and also assist us in ministering to other people. As I said "I bind your hands and feet according to Matt 18:18" the angels instantly restrained the boy and physically held him down. **God had clearly shown me how to use the keys of the kingdom of God!**

Psalm 103:20 "Bless the LORD, you His angels, who excel in strength, who do His word, heeding the voice of His word. ^{21}*Bless the LORD, all you His hosts, you ministers of His, who do His pleasure."*

The Angels are our fellow workers waiting to confirm the commandments that we speak. They are God's commandments and we are putting a voice to them. They will only hearken to God's commandments and not ours. WE MUST PUT A VOICE TO THEM IF WE EXPECT THE ANGELS TO MINISTER FOR US. Notice the angels excel in strength. God sent one Angel to defend Jerusalem and he slew 185,000 solders in one night. It takes a lot of strength to do that! When I spoke the commandment in Matt 18, "I bind your hands and feet," the angel with great strength restrained him. During the deliverance session with the young man, occasionally his hands would come up off the floor a couple of inches and then they would be slammed back to the floor. I knew the angel holding him down was very strong! I knew my days of being fearful of the enemy working through people were over from that day forward!

Many times I have had angels hold violent and disruptive people while I cast out the spirits. That scripture "If God be for you, who can be against you" is a very powerful, comforting truth! You and God are all that is needed as He is your ever present help in time of trouble. The angels represent God! I will share more of these incidents later in the book.

Let me share incidents in the bible where binding and loosing were practiced. Let's look at the Greek definitions again for binding and loosing:

The Greek word to bind is Deo which means to bind, fasten, tie, any sort of binding. As I said before, things that are not permitted in heaven. The Greek word for loose is Luo and means to loosen, unbind, release, or untie…As mentioned before, things that are permitted in heaven.

In the beginning of Jesus ministry the people were trying to kill him by throwing him off a cliff and he turned and walked through the throng of people surrounding him. All he would have had to say was I bind every one of you and the angels would have held each one of them as he passed through their midst. Jesus knew what the keys of the kingdom were as he had them to give to Peter.

Matt 18:18 "*Assuredly, I say to you, whatever you bind on earth will be bound in heaven, and whatever you loose on earth will be loosed in heaven.*" It is critical that God's people understand what the keys are and how to use them correctly. Remember a key inserted or used the wrong way will not work! Have you ever tried to unlock a door at night in the dark and find out you had the wrong key or had it upside down? That is why it is so important that we thoroughly understand how to bind and loose correctly! If you are correctly binding something, you should see an immediate result of that person or thing being bound or tied up. The same is true if you are loosing or untying something. The person or thing should be untied or unrestrained! **If you do not see an immediate result your key could be upside down!**

So many of God's people are repeaters of what they have heard or been taught and have not received the true revelation of God's word concerning the matter. **We must search the scriptures.** Jesus had a short time to teach the principals of binding and loosing to his disciples so he took every opportunity to show them how to properly use the keys.

In Matt 21:17-22 Jesus **bound** a fig tree so that it would never produce fruit again. Within one day of cursing (binding) the tree it had withered and was dying. Jesus knew how to use the keys!

In verse 21 Jesus said we could loose or remove a mountain if we did not doubt in our hearts.

" Now in the morning, as He returned to the city, He was hungry. [19]And seeing a fig tree by the road, He came to it and found nothing on it but leaves, and said to it, "Let no fruit grow on you ever again." Immediately the fig tree withered away. [20]And when the disciples saw it, they marveled, saying, "How did the fig tree wither away so soon?" [21]So Jesus answered and said to them, "Assuredly, I say to you, if you have faith and do not doubt, you will not only do what was done to the fig tree, but also if you say to this mountain, "Be removed and be cast into the sea,' it will be done. [22]And whatever things you ask in prayer, (using the key's properly) *believing, you will receive."*

Another clear principal of us loosing something on earth and believing God will loose the same in the heaven realm is shown in the following passages:

Matt 21:1-6 "now when they drew near Jerusalem, and came to Bethpage, at the Mount of Olives, then Jesus sent two disciples, [2]saying to them, "Go into the village opposite you, and immediately you will find a donkey tied, and a colt with her. Loose them and bring them to Me. [3]And if anyone says anything to you, you shall say, "The Lord has need of them," and immediately he will send them. [4]All this was done that it might be fulfilled which was spoken by the prophet, saying: [5]"Tell the daughter of Zion,   "Behold, your King is coming to you, Lowly, and sitting on a donkey, a colt, the foal of a donkey." [6]So the disciples went and did as Jesus commanded them. The key Jesus gave them was", "The Lord has need of them." Always remember that the keys are obedience to God's commandments! They brought the donkey and the colt, laid their clothes on them, and set Him on them."

The disciples were doing the natural by obeying the instructions Jesus gave them while Father God was working in the supernatural realm to get word to the owners of the animals. God could have given them a dream, vision, or sent angels or other disciples to get word to the owners that the Lord had need of them.

God is well able to do His part well in the Heavenly or invisible realm! As long as we obey the scriptures, God will always do His part (confirm His word.) Luke 13:10-15 is a powerful account of the keys of the kingdom being used by Jesus to loose something on earth (a woman), daughter of Abraham, which implies a woman of faith (a believer)!

Jesus Used the Keys

"[10]Now He was teaching in one of the synagogues on the Sabbath. [11]And behold, there was a woman who had a spirit of infirmity eighteen years, and was bent over and could in no way raise herself up. [12]But when Jesus saw her, He called her to Him and said to her, Woman, you are loosed from your infirmity. [13]And He laid His hands on her, and immediately she was made straight, and glorified God. [14]But the ruler of the synagogue answered with indignation, because Jesus had healed on the Sabbath; and he said to the crowd, "There are six days on which men ought to work; therefore come and be healed on them, and not on the Sabbath day." [15]The Lord then answered him and said, "Hypocrite does not each one of you on the Sabbath loose his ox or donkey from the stall, and lead it away to water it? [16]So ought not this woman, being a daughter of Abraham, whom Satan has bound--think of it--for eighteen years, is loosed from this bond on the Sabbath?"
[17]And when He said these things, all His adversaries were put to shame; and all the multitude rejoiced for all the glorious things that were done by Him."

There are many Christians today that are bound by spirits of infirmities and need to be "loosed" from the bondages Satan has bound them with. We as Christians need to use the keys to the kingdom which Jesus gave us and begin setting the captives free. Look in a medical dictionary and you will be amazed at how many infirmities are listed. **Just think we have keys that can unlock prison doors and let people go free.** People in many churches today would not have been able to set this woman free because of their traditions concerning not believing that Christians can be affected by evil spirits! **We must wake up and begin to do the works that Jesus did; He gave us the keys so**

let's start using them!

Jesus said when I was in prison you visited me. There are many different kinds of prisons besides jail cells! Everywhere Jesus went he was constantly teaching his disciples how to use the keys to the kingdom of God by releasing people that were in bondage.

Jesus Looses Deaf & Dumb Boy

In Mark 7:31-37 *"Again, departing from the region of Tyre and Sidon, He came through the midst of the region of Decapolis to the Sea of Galilee. [32] Then they brought to Him one who was deaf and had an impediment in his speech and they begged Him to put His hand on him. [33] And He took him aside from the multitude, and put His fingers in his ears, and He spat and touched his tongue. [34] Then, looking up to heaven, He sighed, and said to him, "Ephphatha, that is, be opened.* (The same terminology as be loosed). *[35] Immediately his ears were opened, and the impediment of his tongue was loosed, and he spoke plainly. [36] Then He commanded them that they should tell no one; but the more He commanded them, the more widely they proclaimed it. [37] And they were astonished beyond measure, saying, "He has done all things well. He makes both the deaf to hear and the mute to speak."*

If Jesus had not **loosed** the boy he would have stayed in prison (deafness) perhaps the rest of his life. The thief (Satan) has come to steal, kill, and destroy but Jesus came that we might have life and have it more abundantly. We can use the keys of binding and loosing Jesus gave us to enable people to have that abundant life!

God has used me a number of times to heal the deaf. I usually put my fingers in each ear like Jesus did and say "ears be opened." Usually the people are startled when I pull my fingers out of their ears. They describe the event as a sudden popping as the spirits come out releasing their ability to hear normally. My wife Betty and I have been to several services where a minister named Earnest Angley ministered and literally hundreds of deaf people from all over the world received their hearing. He is very gifted in that area of ministry and almost one hundred percent of the time he is able to open every deaf ear!

We took two deaf people with us to his service in Charlotte, NC several years ago and both came back clapping their hands as they listened to gospel music for the first time on the car radio. We were really rejoicing with them as they were experiencing the new sounds for the first time. Jesus said some deaf and dumb spirits would only come out by prayer and fasting so we, as servants of the Lord, need to practice fasting along with our regular prayer life, in order to stay strong in the Lord and in the power of his might!

I played professional baseball in the New York Yankees organization for 10 years as a pitcher. Many times I was used as a relief pitcher in close games so I had to be prepared when called on to "put out the fire." Baseball players, before the season begins, go to Florida for spring training to get in shape so when the season begins they will be ready. Much of our preparation was running and throwing the ball to strengthen our legs and throwing arm. We practiced throwing the ball over different parts of the plate; using fast balls, curves, sliders, and change ups. All of this was teaching us discipline so when the season opened and the real games began, we would be in shape and ready to face any crisis! We as Christians must get in shape if we are to do the works that Jesus did! Prayer and fasting are two good exercises to begin with!

Peter Used the Keys

Jesus did not say if you fast, but when you fast! In the great commission we are instructed to raise the dead! You need the keys to do this! " *[7]And as you go, preach, saying, 'the kingdom of heaven is at hand.' [8]Heal the sick, cleanse the lepers, raise the dead, cast out demons. Freely you have received, freely give.* "

Peter Goes To Joppa with His Keys

Acts 9:36-43 *"At Joppa there was a certain disciple named Tabitha, which is translated Dorcas. This woman was full of* *good works and charitable deeds which she did. ³⁷But it happened in those days that she became sick and died. When they had washed her, they laid her in an upper room. ³⁸And since Lydda was near Joppa, and the disciples had heard that Peter was there, they sent two men to him, imploring him not to delay in coming to them. ³⁹Then Peter arose and went with them. When he had come, they brought him to the upper room. And all the widows stood by him weeping, showing the tunics and garments which Dorcas had made while she was with them. ⁴⁰But Peter put them all out, and knelt down and prayed. And turning to the body he said, "Tabitha, arise." And she opened her eyes, and when she saw Peter she sat up. ⁴¹Then he gave her his hand and lifted her up; and when he had called the saints and widows, he presented her alive. ⁴²And it became known throughout all Joppa, and many believed on the Lord. ⁴³So it was that he stayed many days in Joppa with Simon, a tanner."*

*When peter told Dorcas to arise; the **keys to the kingdom** opened the door to death and she was set free. In Rev 1:18 Jesus said he had the keys to death." ¹⁸I am He who lives, and was dead, and behold, I am alive forevermore. Amen. And I have the keys of Hades and of Death."* **"Whatever you loose on earth (Dorcas was on earth) shall be loosed in heaven, by my Father who is in heaven." It is heaven's will that the dead be raised!**

Jesus gave Peter the keys to the kingdom and he used them many times to demonstrate the spirit and power of God. Many believed after seeing Peter use the keys. They will when they see you use them also!

Peter Loosed Aeneas

Many people today have palsy and the keys to the kingdom are needed to release them! *" ³²Now it came to pass, as Peter went through all parts of the country that he also came down to the saints who dwelt in Lydda. ³³There he found a certain man named Aeneas, who had been bedridden eight years and was paralyzed,. ³⁴And Peter said to him, "Aeneas, Jesus the Christ heals you. Arise and make your bed." Then he arose immediately. ³⁵So all who dwelt at Lydda and Sharon saw him* *and turned to the Lord."* When Peter said arise he was using the **key's to the kingdom** to release Aeneas from palsy. *"Whatever you loose on earth shall be loosed in heaven." In Acts 10:38 how God anointed Jesus of Nazareth with the Holy Spirit and with power, who went about doing good and healing all who were oppressed by the devil, for God was with Him. Jesus had the keys to go about doing good and he has given them to us so we can do the works that he did!*

One day the disciples asked Jesus to increase their faith and he taught them powerful principals of **"Binding and Loosing."**
[5]And the apostles said to the Lord, "Increase our faith." [6]So the Lord said, "If you have faith as a mustard seed, you can say to this mulberry tree, be pulled up by the roots and be planted in the sea, and it would obey you." Jesus was telling them they could **loose a tree.** *[7]And which of you, having a servant plowing or tending sheep, will say to him when he has come in from the field, "Come at once and sit down to eat'? [8]But will he not rather say to him, "Prepare something for my supper, and gird yourself and serve me till I have eaten and drunk, and afterward you will eat and drink'? [9]Does he thank that servant because he did the things that were commanded him? I think not. [10]So likewise you, when you have done all those things which you are commanded, say, "We are unprofitable servants. We have done what was our duty to do*." Imagine people being able to move trees, cancer, palsy, tumors, insanity, and all types of sickness and disease. Jesus said that after we have done these things to say *we are unprofitable servants. We have done what was our duty to do.*

How many men or women of God have you ever heard say aloud I am an unprofitable servant? Jesus said it is our duty to do these things. We need to walk in humility and stop receiving the glory that is due to God and his son Jesus Christ! In John 14:12[-14]"Most assuredly, I say to you, he who believes in me, the works that I do he will do also; and greater works than these he will do, because I go to My Father. [13]And whatever you ask in my name, that I will do, that the Father may be glorified in the Son. [14]If you ask anything in my name, I will do it." Here Jesus is saying whatever we ask of the Father in his name he will do it but only things that will glorify the Father through him. How much glory would we give the Father and Jesus if he did all the mighty signs, wonders, and miracles that the Apostle Paul and other disciples did in the early church? Would we say I am an unprofitable servant, or would we beat our chest and tell the world how we were able to do them with our faith, gifts, fasting, and holy living? The eyes of the Lord search the earth looking for someone whose heart is perfect toward him that he might show himself strong on their behalf. **I believe strong here means humble!** Moses was the meekest man in the earth and look what God was able to do through him in Egypt and in the wilderness! God will do the same things today through people who will do what God expects of all people: **Read it below…**

Micah 6:8 *"He has showed you, O man, what is good. And what does the LORD require of you? To act justly and to love mercy and to walk humbly with your God."* **An incredible incident of using the keys of the kingdom to loose someone bound and guarded securely in prison …**

Church Uses the Keys

" It was about this time that King Herod arrested some who belonged to the church, intending to persecute them. ²He had James, the brother of John, put to death with the sword. ³When he saw that this pleased the Jews; he proceeded to seize Peter also. This happened during the Feast of Unleavened Bread. ⁴After arresting him, he put him in prison, handing him over to be guarded by four squads of four soldiers each. Herod intended to bring him out for public trial after the Passover. ⁵So Peter was kept in prison, but the church was earnestly praying to God for him. ⁶The night before Herod was to bring him to trial, Peter was sleeping between two soldiers, bound with two chains, and sentries stood guard at the entrance. ⁷Suddenly an angel of the Lord appeared and a light shone in the cell. He struck Peter on the side and woke him up. "Quick, get up!" he said, and the chains fell off Peter's wrists. ⁸Then the angel said to him "Put on your clothes and sandals." And Peter did so. "Wrap your cloak around you and follow me," the angel told him. ⁹Peter followed him out of the prison, but he had no idea that what the angel was doing was really happening; he thought he was seeing a vision.

[10]They passed the first and second guards and came to the iron gate leading to the city. It opened for them by itself, and they went through it. When they had walked the length of one street, suddenly the angel left him. [11]Then Peter came to himself and said; "Now I know without a doubt that the Lord sent his angel and rescued me from Herod's clutches and from everything the Jewish people were anticipating." [12]When this had dawned on him, he went to the house of Mary the mother of John, also called Mark, where many people had gathered and were praying. [13]Peter knocked at the outer entrance and a servant girl named Rhoda came to answer the door. [14]When she recognized Peter's voice, she was so overjoyed she ran back without opening it and exclaimed, "Peter is at the door!" [15]"You're out of your mind," they told her. When she kept insisting that it was so, they said, "It must be his angel." [16]But Peter kept on knocking, and when they opened the door and saw him, they were astonished".

Notice the church was loosing him (**using the keys to the kingdom**). They were loosing him on earth and God sent an angel and loosed him in the heavenly realm. The church at first had trouble believing it had worked and doubted that it was really Peter. The keys can be used in many situations to bind and loose things on earth. We will discuss many more applications of these principals working in the old and New Testament. In Psalms 68:6 *"[6]God sets the solitary in families; He brings out those who are bound into prosperity; but the rebellious dwell in a dry land."* There are many references to God bringing out people that are bound.

Paul Binds False Prophet with Blindness

A very dramatic case of binding which will be helpful for us to survive in this evil, violent society in which we live, is when the Apostle Paul bound a false prophet, a sorcerer with blindness. We can do the same thing with the keys of the kingdom of God! God really gave us the right tools to work with in bringing in the harvest. Acts 13:6 *" [12] Now when they had gone through the island to Paphos, they found a certain sorcerer, a false prophet, a Jew whose name was Bar-Jesus, [7] who was with the proconsul, Sergius Paulus, an intelligent man. This man called for Barnabas and Saul and sought to hear the word of God. [8] But Elymas the sorcerer (for so his name is translated) withstood them, seeking to turn the proconsul away from the faith. [9] Then Saul, who also is called Paul, filled with the Holy Spirit, looked intently at him [10] and said, "O full of all deceit and all fraud, you son of the devil, you enemy of all righteousness, will you not cease perverting the straight ways of the Lord? [11] And now, indeed, the hand of the Lord is upon you, and you shall be blind, not seeing the sun for a time." And immediately a dark mist fell on him, and he went around seeking someone to lead him by the hand. [12] Then the proconsul believed, when he saw what had been* **done, being astonished at the teaching of the Lord".** **He Saw the Keys of the Kingdom work!** The false prophet was hindering the work of God so Paul used the key's (hand of the Lord) to bind something on earth which happened to be the sorcerer's eyes. Immediately the blinding was evident as the Sorcerer sought someone to lead him around.

The Lord has used me on four different occasions to teach and minister spiritual warfare in Ireland. On one occasion after an evening service, the whole church went down to the streets and we were preaching and giving testimonies trying to reach some of the multitudes that were in downtown Ireland. As I was giving my testimony to God healing my 1 inch short leg and my chronic back problem, many people had stopped to listen and I could see that God was drawing some of the people by His Holy Spirit. Suddenly this man came up in front of me and started doing every thing imaginable to distract the people from hearing my testimony. He would cover his head with a rag, make funny sounds with his mouth, raise and shake his hands violently in the air. The people's attention was now off the gospel message as he continued interrupting the service. The principal of blinding a person came up out of my spirit but honestly I was afraid to use the keys of the Kingdom as Paul had done. The key I could have used was "**Be blind for a season.**" I have never tried to use that key but I have it if the need arises again. There are many witches, sorcerers, satanists, and false prophets that will try to hinder the work of God by hindering people from hearing the gospel message. God is ready to show himself strong on behalf of the servants that have their hearts toward him and that are not out to build a reputation and kingdom for themselves. Remember how the false prophets in Pharaoh's court opposed Moses and Aaron by performing many miraculous signs and wonders. We face the same situation today and we must be ready to use the keys Jesus gave us to bring in the harvest and bring Glory to his name.

Guatemala Experience

A dramatic story of binding and loosing happened to a local lady we will call Rachael. Here is her story as she tells it.:
"While in Guatemala on a mission trip, my team was sent out into the congregation at the end of the crusade service to minister to the people, as is their custom. We prayed for these dear people, most of who are brokenhearted and in such spiritual bondage, to ancestral witchcraft, incest, alcoholism, sorcery, rejection, poverty, and many other heart rending bondages which Satan has kept their people entrenched in for many years. The spirit of God moves mightily in these revival services. These people, who can't even speak the language that we pray for them in, and can't understand what we say when we pray deliverance over them would begin to manifest as we laid hands on them, rebuking the evil spirits tormenting them. One such young woman, as I prayed for her, began to weep and shake. The Lord revealed deep bondages and many cruel things done to her in her childhood. As the "finger of God" touched on these spirits, she violently shook and screamed waving her arms. Seated next to her was a young mother with an infant in her arms. I saw the fear in her eyes as she tried to shield her baby's head from the woman's flailing arms. At first, I tried to hold her with the help of my intercessor who was trying to protect me. But the girl was incredibly strong due to the manifestation (she was a tiny woman in her late teens, and probably only weighed 110 lbs. at maximum, and I am 5'8" and very strong for a woman, but I couldn't contain her). I then remembered a prophecy I received before going on this trip from Stan Johnson that God was going to show me His strength and power by demonstrating the power

31

of binding someone that I would minister to. I breathed a quick prayer for God's help and commanded her hands to be bound in the name of Jesus. As soon as I spoke the words, her hands came together at the wrist in an "x" formation, just as if her wrists were tied with rope together. My intercessor gasped out loud and looked at me with her eyes as big as saucers, and we both just thanked God for His mighty power. The young woman was still shaking, but God held her firmly in her seat till we finished praying for her."

Elisha Binds an Entire Army with Blindness
2 Kings 6:8-23

Elisha also used the keys to the kingdom blinding an entire army! In this event Elisha had been warning the king of Israel that the King of Syria was planning to ambush them at a certain location and for them not to pass by that way. Many times the king of Syria's plans were thwarted and when they found out Elisha was a prophet that heard what the king was planning in his bedchamber, he sent his army to arrest Elisha. Read the entire event as follows. "*[8]Now the king of Syria was making war against Israel; and he consulted with his servants, saying, "My camp will be in such and such a place." [9]And the man of God sent to the king of Israel, saying, "Beware that you do not pass this place, for the Syrians are coming down there." [10]Then the king of Israel sent someone to the place of which the man of God had told him. Thus he warned him, and he was watchful there, not just once or twice. [11]Therefore the heart of the king of Syria was greatly troubled by this thing; and he called his servants and said to them, "Will you not show me which of us is for the king of Israel?" [12]And one of his servants said, "None, my lord, O king; but Elisha, the prophet who is in Israel, tells the king of Israel the words that you speak in your bedroom." [13]So he said, "Go and see where he is, that I may send and get him." And it was told him, saying, "Surely he is in Dothan." [14]Therefore he sent horses and chariots and a great army there and they came by night and surrounded the city. [15]And when the servant of the man of God arose early and went out, there was an army,*

surrounding the city with horses and chariots. And his servant said to him, "Alas, my master!
What shall we do?" So he answered do not fear, for those who are with us are more than those who are with them. ^{16}So he answered, "Do not fear, for those who are with us are more than they that be with them. ^{17}And Elisha prayed, and said, "LORD, I pray, open his eyes that he may see." Then the LORD opened the eyes of the young man, and he saw. And behold, the mountain was full of horses and chariots of fire round about Elisha. ^{18}So when the Syrians came down to him, Elisha prayed to the LORD, and said, "Strike this people, I pray, with blindness." And He struck them with blindness according to the word of Elisha. Now Elisha said to them, "This is not the way, nor is this the city. Follow me, and I will bring you to the man whom you seek." But he led them to Samaria.^{20}So it was, when they had come to Samaria, that Elisha said, "LORD, open the eyes of these men that they may see." And the LORD opened their eyes, and they saw; and there they were, inside Samaria! ^{21}Now when the king of Israel saw them, he said to Elisha, "My father, shall I kill them? Shall I kill them?" ^{22}But he answered, "You shall not kill them. Would you kill those whom you have taken captive with your sword and your bow? Set food and water before them that they may eat and drink and go to their master." ^{23}Then he prepared a great feast for them; and after they ate and drank, he sent them away and they went to their master. So the bands of Syrian raiders came no more into the land of Israel." Elisha used the keys of the kingdom to blind an entire army! Isn't it comforting to know that a servant of the Lord could face and defeat an entire army today with the keys of the kingdom and knowing how to use them!

Homosexuals Bound With Blindness

Another instance of binding people's eyes with blindness happened when the angels came to Lot's house to tell him he must leave the city so God's judgment could be on the wicked city that had given themselves over to sexual sins of Homosexuality and Lesbianism. *Ezek 16:49-50, "this was the iniquity of your sister Sodom: She and her daughter had pride, fullness of food, and abundance of idleness; neither did she strengthen the hand of the poor and needy. [50]And they were haughty and committed abomination before me; therefore I took them away as I saw fit."* The church today needs to remember there are other sins God judged Sodom for besides sexual sins! The scriptures also say that the townspeople came to Lot's door demanding what they thought were two men, not knowing that they were angels, to be brought forth that they could have perverted sexual acts with them. The angels used the keys to the Kingdom and bound every one of them with blindness! Remember to use the keys of binding and loosing if someone is attempting to rape or harm you. It would be hard for someone to rape or assault you if they could not see! Read the entire account below. *"Now the two angels came to Sodom in the evening, and Lot was sitting in the gate of Sodom. When Lot saw them, he rose to meet them, and he bowed himself with his face toward the ground. [2]And he said, "Here now, my lords, please turn in to your servants house, and spend the night, and wash your feet; then you may rise early and go on your way. And they said "no, but we will spend the night in the open square." But he insisted strongly; so they turned in to him and entered his house. Then he made them a feast, and baked unleavened bread, and they ate. [4]Now before they lay down, the men of the city, the men of Sodom, both old and young, all the people from every quarter, surrounded the house. [5]And they called to Lot and said to him, "Where are the men who came to you tonight? Bring them out to us that we may know them carnally." [6]So Lot went out to them through the doorway shut the door behind him, [7]and said, "Please, my brethren, do not do so wickedly! [8]See now, I have two daughters who have not known a man; please, let me bring them out to you, and you may do to them as you wish; only do nothing to these men, since this is the reason they have come under the shadow of my roof." [9]And they said, "Stand back!" Then they said, "This one came in to stay here, and he keeps acting as a judge; now we will deal worse with you than with them." So they pressed hard against the man Lot, and came near to break down the door. [10]But the men reached out their hands and pulled Lot into the house with them, and shut the door. [11]And they struck the men who were at the doorway of the house with* *blindness, both small and great, so that they became weary trying to find the door. ¹²Then the men said to Lot, "Have you anyone else here? Son-in-law, your sons, your daughters, and whomever you have in the city--take them out of this place! ¹³For we will destroy this place, because the outcry against them has grown great before the face of the LORD, and the LORD has sent us to destroy it." ¹⁴So Lot went out and spoke to his sons-in-law, who had married his daughters, and said, "Get up, get out of this place; for the LORD will destroy this city!" But to his sons-in-law he seemed to be joking. ¹⁵When the morning dawned, the angels urged Lot to hurry, saying, "Arise, take your wife and your two daughters who are here, lest you be consumed in the punishment of the city." ¹⁶And while he lingered, the men took hold of his hand, his wife's hand, and the hands of his two daughters, the LORD being merciful to him, and they brought him out and set him outside the city. ¹⁷So it came to pass, when they had brought them outside, that he said, "Escape for your life! Do not look behind you nor stay anywhere in the plain. Escape to the mountains, lest you be destroyed." ¹⁸Then Lot said to them, "Please, no, my lords! ¹⁹Indeed now, your servant has found favor in your sight, and you have increased your mercy which you have shown me by saving my life; but I cannot escape to the mountains, lest some evil overtake me and I die. ²⁰See now, this city is near enough to flee to, and it is a little one; please let me escape there (is it not a little one?) and my soul shall live." ²¹And he said to him, "See, I have favored you concerning this thing also, in that I will not overthrow this city for which you have spoken. ²²Hurry, escape there. For I cannot do anything until you arrive there." Therefore the name of the city was called Zoar."*

Sodom & Gomorrah Destroyed

"The sun had risen upon the earth when Lot entered Zoar. ²⁴Then the LORD rained brimstone and fire on Sodom and Gomorrah, from the LORD out of the heavens. ²⁵So He overthrew those cities, all the plain, all the inhabitants of the cities, and what grew on the ground. ²⁶But his wife looked back behind him and

she became a pillar of salt. [27]And Abraham went early in the morning to the place where he had stood before the LORD. [28]Then he looked toward Sodom and Gomorrah, and toward all the land of the plain; and he saw, and behold, the smoke of the land which went up like the smoke of a furnace. [29]And it came to pass, when God destroyed the cities of the plain, that God remembered Abraham, and sent Lot out of the midst of the overthrow, when He overthrew the cities in which Lot had dwelt." God's people will need to use these keys as we are fast approaching the wickedness that once prevailed in the earth. The scriptures teach that what once has happened before is happening now! It will continue to be more profound as sin is closer to being complete.

Sin Is Nearing Completion

In Romans chapter 1 it says that people, who once knew God, did not want to retain God in their knowledge and God gave them over to their own evil desires and they were filled with all unrighteousness. (**That is total darkness or all evil**) "*For I am not ashamed of the gospel of Christ, for it is the power of God to salvation for everyone who believes, for the Jew first and also for the Greek. [17]For in it the righteousness of God is revealed from faith to faith; as it is written, "The just shall live by faith."*"

God's Wrath on Unrighteousness

"*For the wrath of God is revealed from heaven against all ungodliness and unrighteousness of men, who suppress the truth in unrighteousness, [19]because what may be known of God is manifest in them, for God has shown it to them. [20]For since the creation of the world His invisible attributes are clearly seen, being understood by the things that are made, even His eternal power and Godhead, so that they are without excuse, [21]because, although they knew God, they did not glorify Him as God, nor were thankful, but became futile in their thoughts, and their foolish hearts were darkened. [22]Professing to be wise, they became fools, [23]and changed the glory of the incorruptible God into an image made like corruptible man--and birds and four-footed animals and creeping things. [24]Therefore God also gave them up to uncleanness, in the lusts of their hearts, to dishonor their bodies among themselves; [25]who exchanged the truth of God for the lie, and worshiped and served the creature rather than the Creator, who is blessed forever. Amen. [26]For this reason God gave them up to vile passions. For even their women exchanged the natural use for what is against nature. [27]Likewise also the men, leaving the natural use of the woman, burned in their lust for one another, men with men committing what is shameful, and receiving in themselves the penalty of their error which was due. [28]And even as they did not like to retain God in their knowledge, God gave them over to a debased mind, to do those things which are not fitting; [29]being filled with all unrighteousness, sexual immorality, wickedness, covetousness, maliciousness; full of envy, murder, strife, deceit, evil-mindedness; they are whisperers, [30]backbiters, haters of God, violent, proud, boasters, inventors of evil things, disobedient to parents, [31]undiscerning, untrustworthy, unloving, unforgiving, unmerciful; [32]who, knowing the righteous judgment of God, that those who practice such things are deserving of death, not only do the same but also approve of those who practice them."*

Notice how people today do not want anything to do with God! They want to remove the 10 commandments; they want to take Christ out of Christmas, prayer out of our schools. This is the spirit of anti-Christ that Paul said would increase in the last days! The spirit of anti-Christ is anything that opposes or wants to replace Christ. The Apostle Paul said nearly 2,000 years ago that this spirit was at work in his day and it would increase in the last days. **What a sign that we are living in those days!** In Judges 21:25 God describes these people who will not submit to God's laws and walk in his ways. *"[25]In those days there was no king in Israel; everyone did what was right in his own eyes."* Can you imagine living in a society where people would accept no restraints placed on them! Are we not seeing this happening in people today? **These Are GOD HATERS AT WORK!** They do not want any absolutes or anyone ruling over them!

The Lions Mouth Bound

The story of Daniel in the lion's den is another example of binding and loosing that should give us much confidence if we are ever thrown into a lion's den for our faith as the Prophet Daniel was. Daniel knew God and was familiar with the keys of the kingdom. He refused to stop bowing down and worshiping his God and because of the kings decree, he was thrown in the Lions den as punishment The entire account is as follows Daniel 6, *" ¹It pleased Darius to set over the kingdom one hundred and twenty princes, to be over the whole kingdom; ²and over these, three governors, of whom Daniel was one, that the princes might give account to them, so that the king would suffer no loss. ³Then this Daniel distinguished himself above the governors and princes, because an excellent spirit was in him; and the king gave thought to setting him over the whole realm. ⁴So the governors and princes sought to find some charge against Daniel concerning the kingdom; but they could find no charge or fault, because he was faithful; nor was there any error or fault found in him. ⁵Then these men said, "We shall not find any charge against this Daniel unless we find it against him concerning the law of his God.". So these governors and satraps thronged before the king, and said thus to him: "King Darius, live forever! ⁷All the governors of the kingdom, the administrators and princes, the counselors and advisors, have consulted together to establish a royal statute and to make a firm decree, that whoever petitions any god or man for thirty days, except you, O king, shall be cast into the den of lions. ⁸Now, O king, establish the decree and sign the writing, so that it cannot be changed, according to the law of the Medes and Persians, which does not alter." ⁹Therefore King Darius signed the written decree. ¹⁰Now when Daniel knew that the writing was signed, he went home. And in his upper room, with his windows open toward Jerusalem, he knelt down on his knees three times that day, and prayed and gave thanks before his God, as was his*

custom since early days. [11]Then these men assembled and found Daniel praying and making supplication before his God. [12]And they went before the king and spoke concerning the king's decree: "Have you not signed a decree that every man who petitions any god or man within thirty days, except you, O king, shall be cast into the den of lions?" The king answered and said, "The thing is true, according to the law of the Medes and Persians, which does not alter." [13]So they answered and said before the king, "That Daniel, who is one of the captives from Judah, does not show due regard for you, O king, or for the decree that you have signed, but makes his petition three times a day." [14]And the king, when he heard these words, was greatly displeased with himself, and set his heart on Daniel to deliver him; and he labored till the going down of the sun to deliver him. [15]Then these men approached the king, and said to the king, "Know, O king, that it is the law of the Medes and Persians that no decree or statute which the king establishes may be changed." [16]So the king gave the command and they brought Daniel and cast him into the den of lions. But the king spoke, saying to Daniel, "Your God, whom you serve continually, He will deliver you." [17]Then a stone was brought and laid on the mouth of the den, and the king sealed it with his own signet ring and with the signets of his lords, that the purpose concerning Daniel might not be changed"

Daniel Saved from the Lions

[18]Now the king went to his palace and spent the night fasting; and no musicians were brought before him. Also his sleep went from him. [19]Then the king arose very early in the morning and went in haste to the den of lions. [20]And when he came to the den, he cried out with a lamenting voice to Daniel. The king spoke, saying to Daniel, "Daniel, servant of the living God, has your God, whom you serve continually, been able to deliver you from the lions?" [21]Then Daniel said to the king, "O king, live forever! [22]My God sent His angel and shut the lions' mouths, so that they have not hurt me, because I was found innocent before Him; and also, O king, I have done no wrong before you." [23]Now the king was exceedingly glad for him, and commanded that they should

take Daniel up out of the den. So Daniel was taken up out of the den, and no injury whatever was found on him, because he believed in his God." **We must believe in our God and the keys He has given us to bind & loose!**

Darius Honors God

"And the king gave the command, and they brought those men, who had accused Daniel, and they cast them into the den of lions--them, their children, and their wives; and the lions overpowered them, and broke all their bones in pieces before they ever came to the bottom of the den [25]Then King Darius wrote: to all peoples, nations, and languages that dwell in all the earth: Peace be multiplied to you. [26]I make a decree that in every dominion of my kingdom men must tremble and fear before the God of Daniel. For He is the living God, and steadfast forever; His kingdom is the one which shall not be destroyed, and His dominion shall endure to the end. [27]He delivers and rescues and He work signs and wonders in heaven and on earth, who has delivered Daniel from the power of the lions. [28]So this Daniel prospered in the reign of Darius and in the reign of Cyrus the Persian." **Having and knowing how to use the keys of the kingdom can not only save your life, but like Daniel, can cause you to be promoted!**

Jesus Binds Wind & Waves

"Whatever" we bind on earth includes a lot of things so let's look at a situation Jesus used to teach the disciples a powerful lesson on other possibilities for using the keys of the kingdom. Mark 4:35-41 "[35]On the same day, when evening had come; He said to them, "Let us cross over to the other side." [36]Now when they had left the multitude, they took Him along in the boat as He was. And other little boats were also with Him. [37]And a great windstorm arose and the waves beat into the boat, so that it was already filling. [38]But He was in the stern, asleep on a pillow. And they awoke Him and said to Him, "Teacher, do you not care that we are perishing?" [39]Then He arose and rebuked the wind, and said to the sea, "Peace, be still!" And the wind ceased and there was a great calm. [40]But He said to them, "Why are you so fearful? How is it that you have no faith?" [41]And they feared exceedingly, and said to one another, "Who can this be, that even the wind and the sea obey Him!" The Hebrew word means He muffled the wind! The same terminology as he bound the wind. Imagine what Jesus is saying. We can bind the wind and the sea with our keys.

Notice two of their problems, the fear and their lack of faith. These two hindrances can also keep us from experiencing the supernatural! Just think of the possibilities with all the volatile weather, tornadoes, raging seas, etc. Over the years my wife Betty and I have bound the rain at various times and have seen amazing results as we traveled and needed to unload our car when we would arrive at a church or motel. God says we have not because we ask not. Start asking and exercising your faith as your Heavenly Father wants to take you up higher! We had better keep our keys handy for whatever may come as the days of sorrow continue. God said that He would never leave or forsake His people but would be with them until the end of the age. God said his people perish for lack of knowledge so we should be seeking truth revealed in His word if we desire to live a long and productive life. "Iron sharpens iron," so lets sharpen each other by submitting to one another until we all come into the unity of the faith unto a perfect man. Heb 11:32-40 in this famous faith chapter there are several instances where the keys to the kingdom (**binding and loosing**) were used. "[32]*And what more shall I say? For the time would fail me to tell of Gideon and Barak and Samson and Jephthah, also of David and Samuel and the prophets: [33]who through faith subdued kingdoms, worked righteousness, obtained promises, stopped the mouths of lions, [34]quenched the violence of fire, escaped the edge of the sword, out of weakness were made strong, became valiant in battle, turned to flight the armies of the aliens. [35]Women received their dead raised to life again. Others were tortured, not accepting deliverance, that they might obtain a better resurrection. [36]Still others had trial of mocking and scourging, yes, and of chains and imprisonment. [37]They were stoned, they were sawn in two, were tempted, and were slain with the sword.*

They wandered about in sheepskins and goatskins, being destitute, afflicted, tormented-- [38]of whom the world was not worthy. They wandered in deserts and mountains, in dens and caves of the earth. [39]And all these, having obtained a good testimony through faith, did not receive the promise, [40]God having provided something better for us, apart from us that they should not be made perfect subdued kingdoms...Stopped the mouth of Lions (binding them)... Quenched the violence of fire (binding the fire). Escaped the edge of the sword (binding their enemies)."

Many Times The Keys Worked For Me.

I taught this binding and loosing doctrine several years ago in the Washington, DC area to a group of Christians who were hungry for the revelation of God's word. A teenager was present that worked at a veterinary business in the area. His job was to take the animals out of their cage and put them on the grooming table. As he was ready to take this aggressive dog out of his cage, the dog started to threaten him. He said the teaching he had learned from me came back to his memory and he said to the dog "I bind you in Jesus name according to Matt 18". He said the dog acted like it was frozen stiff and was no threat to him in that condition. He was amazed to see God's power work as he used the keys to the kingdom of God! He said when the owners arrived to pick up their dog he was ready to bind the dog again to see God's power at work. He said the Lord spoke to him and said you do not need to do that again, but have the owners take their dog out of the cage for you. God did not want him to start binding things when it was not needful. **This principal will work when and only if it is needed.**

Another Dog Is Bound

A very well known Pastor tells of an experience he had binding a dog that saved a man from certain death. As he was driving up to a house where he planned a visit, this woman came running

out of the house screaming "this dog is killing my husband!"
This very large German shepherd had been viciously attacking
her husband in the back yard and had severely damaged his arm,
tearing flesh from his shoulder down to his elbow exposing
much of the bone; he had also suffered considerable blood loss.
The man had managed to lean against this tree where the dog
was poised and ready to continue the attack, which would
certainly have been fatal. The minister picked up a broom and a
chair and started to work his way towards the man to try and
rescue him. The Holy Spirit said "bind" him. The minister said
he did not understand how he could bind a dog but responded
with "I bind you in Jesus name." The dog appeared to freeze and
was unable to move giving him a chance to assist the man who
fainted in his arms. He applied a tourniquet to stop the bleeding
before the ambulance arrived and they were barely able to save
the mans life. Thank God for the keys to be able to bind things
on earth!

Pastor Binds Man in Chair

**We are going to need the keys! Virgil Mobley, a pastor
friend of mine in Tylersport, Pa., where I have ministered
many times over the years, wrote me the following testimony
concerning the doctrine of Binding & Loosing I taught in his
church: "I just wanted you to know that over the years that
you have been coming to Victory Church, I have learned a
lot from you and Betty. I will never forget the time you told
about a man who came for deliverance and he started
kicking out of control, and you said "I tie the strong man up
in the name of Jesus," and he calmed down right away.
Because of the teachings you gave at Victory, I had a man
who came to get delivered and as I was praying for him, he
got out of control and said he was going to throw me out the
window. I knew I had to do something because that evil spirit
started to act up really strong. Then I said "I tie the strong
man up in the name of Jesus" and immediately this man was
unable to move. He just sat there! I told the man I would
release him when the Lord told me to. It was for about 15
minutes that he sat there and could not move. Praise the**

Lord, He is right on time.

    God bless,
    Pastor Virgil

That was a copy of the letter he wrote me describing the event that took place! The keys of the Kingdom are for God's people to use when they are needed!

Many testimonies where this doctrine has been used have greatly encouraged me to write this book that God's people will have a good understanding of the power of using the keys to the kingdom.

Woman Binds Abusive Husband

A woman gave me this testimony of how the Lord protected her from her intoxicated husband who was ready to leave for work. At the door he was ready to hit her in his fit of anger. As he pulled back his clenched fist to strike her she said "I bind you in Jesus name according to Matt 18!" Instantly he froze in that position and glared at her in unbelief. As she stood there smiling at him she said, "if you promise to stop abusing me I will loose you and let you go to work." He sheepishly looked at her and nodded yes he would behave. Immediately he was loosed and hurriedly left for work.

She said it was not long after that incident before he left her since he was unwilling to turn to God and was no longer able to control her with physical abuse and fear.

God is with His people to protect us, but we must learn to use the keys to the kingdom when they are needed.

Violent man in Ireland Bound

On one of my trips to Ireland, while teaching spiritual warfare and ministering to the people, God let me have an exciting, dramatic experience in one of the meetings.

I had been going around this large room with many people sitting waiting for me to lay hands and pray over them. When I came to this one man sitting with his head looking down, I asked him if I could pray for him. He nodded that it was ok and I proceeded to put my hands on his head and began praying in the Spirit. Suddenly he jumped straight up out of his chair and raising both clinched fists high above his head screamed, "I hate you!" His face was flushed with rage and you could see the devil manifesting in his face. I instantly said "I bind your hands in Jesus name according to Matt 18." His hands were held over his head for at least five minutes while I told him how much Jesus loved him and wanted him to go free from the evil working in and through his life. I proceeded to explain to him that he could be released and free to serve the Lord and do his will.

After several minutes of sharing the good news of the gospel with his hands still "frozen" above his head, I asked him if he wanted to repent and go free. He nodded yes and I said "I loose you in Jesus name" and instantly, his hands were released and he fell to the floor on his knees repenting.

I did not know at the time that he had been so involved with the sins of the world, such as homosexuality, group sex, the occult, and witchcraft. As the spirits were coming out of him his whole countenance changed before our eyes and he started speaking in tongues as he was baptized with the Holy Spirit and fire that John the Baptist said was **available to all believers**.

Needless to say everyone, including the angels, rejoiced at the working of God in his life.

As I have been teaching, I bound the strong man, and spoiled his house, taking the goods (spirits) out using the keys of the kingdom Jesus gave Peter!

When the strong man is bound, the spirits can not use the person to harm you.

Notice that I was not binding Satan, or his spirits, but only the man so I could get the spirits out of him. **Jesus either cast the spirits out of a person, or loosed the person from the spirits.** The Lord told me one time that I could not improve on his methods of ministry and I was to follow his example.

Woman bound Hand and Foot

My wife Betty and I were ministering in a church in Virginia. After the teaching, as we prayed for this one lady, she became very violent and the spirit threw her to the floor and she began to kick and frail her arms around.

The Lord said to bind her hand and foot with one single command, and instantly her hands and feet were restrained as if an invisible rope had bound her. The Holy Spirit then through the gift of discernment told us what to cast out in order to set her free. The whole church rejoiced as we saw the power of God manifest in delivering this woman.

As the church we are suppose to be demonstrating the spirit and power of God.

In 1st Corith 1:4-5 *"and my speech and my preaching were not with persuasive words of human wisdom, but in demonstration of the Spirit and of power, [5]that your faith should not be in the wisdom of men but in the power of God"*

Imagine a famous pianist explaining how a piano works and sounds to someone that has never seen or heard one played. After the explanation he could demonstrate all the wonderful sounds and effects to thrill all the people present. In a similiar manner we are to demonstrate the spirit and power of God. The whole great commission requires that the word and power be demonstrated to help people believe. Many people believed when the signs and wonders were performed in the early church.

Nicodemus told Jesus that because of the works that he did, it proved that God was with him! The world needs to see by our demonstrating the Holy Spirit and power that God is with us!

A Week in Missouri!

One of the most adventurous times of using the keys of the kingdom was a week in a town in Missouri, the state that says "I am from Missouri, show me." God was ready to show me things I knew not of.

This rather large church invited Betty and me to come and minister deliverance to seventeen of their people who were in desperate need of help. Upon arriving they took us to a home in the country where the people were to come the following morning for deliverance and restoration.

Two of the church elders that were beginning to learn how to minister deliverance were to stay there with us that night and help us prepare for the ministry the following morning. Just prior to us turning in for the night two of the church people brought a rather distraught girl in her mid twenties who had her black motorcycle leather outfit on. She was barely coherent and her eyes were rolling back in her head with only the whites of her eyes showing. This was a clear sign of demonic oppression. She was physically violent and the people had to restrain her on the couch. They wanted us to deliver her then, but Satan's plan was to wear us out so we would not be effective the following morning. I explained this to everyone and they asked me what they were to do with this girl until the morning ministry. Spontaneously I said to the girl, "I bind you to that couch you are on until tomorrow morning." The people present asked if that was going to work. I said "I just used one of the keys of the kingdom which is the binding and loosing principals." Needless to say I had never bound anyone to a couch so by morning I was ready for anything.

To my amazement the next morning the girl was still on the couch rubbing her eyes as she was waking up. I had breakfast and noticed she stayed on the couch the entire time not even getting up or asking for a cup of coffee.

The 17 people we were to teach and minister to were all seated and ready for the session to begin. With my bible open in my hands ready to teach the word, suddenly the Hell's angels' girl on the couch said, "I need to go to the bathroom." I said "go ahead and I will wait until you come back to start." Much to my astonishment she said, "I can not get up off the couch." Wow! She was still bound to the couch! I said "I loose you in Jesus name according to Matt 18." At this command she was instantly released and was able to walk to the bathroom. This event was way beyond what I could hope, ask, or think! What had happened was far above my level of faith. This just shows the possibilities of using the keys to the kingdom of God that Jesus made available to us.

This girl had given much place to Satan's kingdom - I was soon to find out that she had been one of the "Hell's Angels" motorcycle gang, had experienced group sex with the bikers, been involved with witchcraft, sorcery, and many other sins that are too numerous to name. She was full of the world!

Many times as the word of God was being taught, the evil spirits in her would violently manifest, and many times through that week of ministry I used the keys to bind her (the strong man) until the spirits were cast out. She along with the others were greatly changed during that week of ministry. God taught me many things that week!

Jesus said that the ministry of deliverance was the working of miracles and we saw many miracles that week as a result of the people going free!

Miracles are for God's people and not the devils children! The church of the Lord Jesus Christ needs to wake up and realize what belongs to God's people - **Deliverance is the children's bread!**

The Demoniac in My Car

God puts us in situations to try our faith so that we might get stronger and more confident in His principles and precepts.

Several years ago I was returning from a ministry trip up in the New England area and on my way south I stopped in a church I had heard about to check it out. After the sermon had concluded a man approached the front of the church and asked for prayer from the elders. As they began to pray for him he became extremely violent and began pushing and shoving the people trying to help him. As they continued praying he started throwing metal chairs around the church and became so unruly that the Elders backed off and said they would not continue but would close the service and go home.

During the violent ordeal I was trying to share with the Elders how to bind the man but they completely ignored my advice telling me that they knew what to do. They were trying to bind Satan and everything except the "strong man."

Jesus said to <u>first</u> bind the strong man and then you can spoil his house by taking the goods out of his house. That man was strong because of the evil spirits in him.

As the church was being closed I engaged the man in

conversation and much to my surprise he asked me if he could get a ride with me heading south. He had hitchhiked to this church for his deliverance and needless to say, he was terribly disappointed and downcast at the results he had just experienced.

As we drove south on the highway, he was in the front passenger seat and in our conversation I asked him how he had become such a violent, aggressive person. He told me a horrible story that I will attempt to relate to you:

He had made an appointment with two ministers who were to "help" him find God, peace, and purpose for his life. He said the ministers had him undress and lay on this table in the church office. He described a very disgusting, ceremonial cleansing they performed on him. He described something like a spiritual wedge being driven in his head as they were massaging his body and doing a so called sanctification or cleansing on him. He said that was the first time he had ever been in any kind of church and did not know what to expect.

I was shocked to hear this kind of deception and seduction being used to destroy people seeking a relationship with God through our Lord Jesus Christ.

Jesus did warn us of false Apostles, false prophets, deceitful workers, and some people among us being enemies of our Lord Jesus Christ. Jesus will say to many in the Day of Judgment *"depart from me ye workers of iniquity, into the fire prepared for the devil and his Angels."* Jesus also said before we would offend one of these little ones, we would be better off to put a millstone around our neck and drown ourselves in the sea!

People that stand in the office of a minister had better take the position seriously and take care of God's sheep according to the instructions God has clearly laid out for us in the scriptures.

A strong warning God gives in Hosea 4:6 *"⁶My people are destroyed for lack of knowledge. Because you have rejected knowledge, I also will reject you from being my priest; because you have forgotten the law of your God, I also will forget your children."*

After his sharing of this horrible experience with the two ministers, and having observed the demonic strongholds being stirred up in him at the church, I knew that I had to bind him (the strong man) before attempting any type of ministry. As many times before in ministering to this type of potentially violent person, I said "I bind you in Jesus name according to Matt 18." Instantly he stiffened and leaned slightly forward as the spirits in him began to manifest. I led him in a prayer forgiving the two men that had brought this terrible mental and physical illness upon him and as that wedge of bondage began to release him, he said his head felt like it would explode.

As I called out the spirits revealed to me by the Holy Spirit, he remained restrained and was not able to do any damage to me or my car. I was driving down the highway during the entire event and was not afraid or fearful of what he might do. "*If God be for us, who can be against us.*" God's angels are exceedingly strong and powerful! They held him in that front seat until the captive was set free. He said the sinner's prayer and was filled with the Holy Spirit and prayed in his prayer language before we stopped for the night.

He was truly a changed person by the power of God and the spirit of Jesus Christ! **Thank God for the keys to bind and loose!**

God is our shield and Fortress

In spiritual warfare it is important to understand where the shield and fortress of God is located because this is our place of safety!

God's Secret Place (Psalm 91)

One day I was leaving a home in our community and a lady came rushing up to me out of breath saying "I saw you ministering at a prayer meeting recently and I need your help desperately." My husband is an alcoholic and is having withdrawal pains. Would you come and pray for him?"

She lived next door and she led me into her house and her husband was literally shaking from the past effects of alcohol addiction.

I asked him if he had ever accepted Jesus Christ as his Lord and Savior. He assured me that he had, but was in a backslidden condition and away from God.

Knowing this, I asked if he was willing to repent and come

back to God and live for him. He agreed and I had him kneel before this piano bench while I led him in the sinner's prayer. As we were praying, I was shocked as he grabbed my trousers leg and began to twist my pants in an aggressive manner. This was in the middle of the prayer! I told him to stop in Jesus name and immediately he stopped, however he continued to hold on to my pant leg with a fistful of my pants in his hand. I then ordered him to release my pants in Jesus name and he did so.

His wife who was sitting close by said "don't hurt Mr. Johnson because he is a nice man." Without hesitation I said "he cannot hurt me because God is my shield and my fortress, in Him will I trust." I felt a strong presence come at this time between this man and myself. He sensed it too and reached out to feel it with his hand. His hand was able to come as close as six inches from my leg but his hand would abruptly stop as if there was an invisible shield there. He would pull his hand back and look at it and then would thrust it again trying to touch my leg. It was not in an aggressive manner but a curiosity as to what was happening. The third try was the same and as he pulled back his hand he said to his wife, "I could touch him a few minutes ago but I cannot touch him now." What boldness I felt at this point, knowing I could cast out the spirits but he could not touch me! Needless to say we had church!

Examine my experience with the word of God.

*"He who dwells in the **secret place** of the Most High Shall abide under the shadow of the Almighty. [2]I will say of the LORD, "He is my refuge and my fortress; My God, in Him I will trust." [3]Surely He shall deliver you from the snare of the fowler and from the perilous pestilence. [4]He shall cover you with His feathers, and under His wings you shall take refuge; His truth shall be your shield and buckler. [5]You shall not be afraid of the terror by night, Nor of the arrow that flies by day, [6]Nor of the pestilence that walks in darkness, Nor of the destruction that lays waste at noonday. A thousand may fall at your side, and ten thousand at your right hand; But it shall not come near you. [8]Only with your eyes shall you look, and see the reward of the wicked. [9]Because you have made the LORD, who is my refuge,*

Even the Most High, your dwelling place, [10]No evil shall befall you, Nor shall any plague come near your dwelling; [11]For He shall give His angels charge over you, To keep you in all your ways. [12]In their hands they shall bear you up, Lest you dash your foot against a stone. [13]You shall tread upon the lion and the cobra, the young lion and the serpent you shall trample underfoot. [14]"Because he has set his love upon me, therefore I will deliver him; I will set him on high, because he has known my name. [15]He shall call upon me, and I will answer him; I will be with him in trouble; I will deliver him and honor him. [16]With long life I will satisfy him, and show him my salvation."
In verse 2   [2]I will say of the LORD, "He is my refuge and my fortress; My God, in Him I will trust." (Psalms 91).

Notice what we have to say! When you need a shield or fortress be sure and say what is stated in verse 2. I personally believe that my protection was an angel that is always with me to protect me.

My shield was activated when I said what was written in the word. A good scripture that confirms this is *"[20]Bless the LORD, you His angels, who excel in strength, who **do His word,** Heeding the **voice of His word.***" **We put the voice to <u>his word!</u>**

Another good scripture that would apply to this. is found in Mark 11:22-24, "So *Jesus answered and aid to them "Have faith in God. [23]For assuredly, I say to you, whoever says to this mountain, "Be removed and be cast into the sea,' and does not doubt in his heart, but believes that those things he says will be done, he will have whatever he says.*
[24]Therefore I say to you, whatever things you ask when you pray, believe that you receive them, and you will have them."
It is important for us to speak the word when you want something to happen!
In Mark 16:20 and they went out and preached everywhere, the Lord working with them and confirming the word through the accompanying signs. Amen.

We must speak the word if we expect the word to be

confirmed!

The Fiery Furnace

In Daniel 3:17-18 the three Hebrew children were in that safe, secret place because of their confession of God's promise to deliver.

King Nebuchadnezzar was demanding the three Hebrew children to bow down to the gold image and worship it or be thrown into a fiery furnace and be destroyed. The Hebrew children answered as follows:

" *[17]If that is the case, our God whom we serve is able to deliver us from the burning fiery furnace, and He will deliver us from your hand, O king. [18]But if not, let it be known to you, O king, that we do not serve your gods, nor will we worship the gold image which you have set up."*

They said God whom they served was able to deliver them and he would deliver them out of the king's hand.

That kind of confession puts God's Angels into action! Remember they hearken to the voice of His commandments! Find God's commandments and speak them. **You provide the voice!**

We Can Bind Kings and Nobles

God give us His wisdom (keys) to bind Kings and nobles but many people would say it was foolish and untraditional to obey that portion of the scriptures.

Are you willing to do the following to bind your enemies?

"[1] Praise the LORD! Sing to the LORD a new song, And His praise in the assembly of saints. [2]Let Israel rejoice in their Maker; Let the children of Zion be joyful in their King. [3]Let them praise His name with the dance; Let them sing praises to Him with the timbrel and harp. [4]For the LORD takes pleasure in His people; He will beautify the humble with salvation. [5]Let the saints be joyful in glory; Let them sing aloud on their beds. [6]Let the high praises of God be in their mouth, and a two-edged sword in their hand, [7]To execute vengeance on the nations, and punishments on the peoples; [8]To bind their kings with chains, and their nobles with fetters of iron; [9]To execute on them the written judgment-- This honor have all His saints. Praise the LORD!" (Psalms 149:1-9).

If you are ashamed or embarrassed to lift your hands in worship and praise to our Lord, you are bound, whether by tradition or your fleshly, carnal nature. He was not ashamed to lift His hands on a cross for you and lay down His life so you could be saved and live forever.

If your church does not allow that type of worship, I would make a change where the church is not bound! We must decide who we are going to please - God or our church!

If you are not willing to practice the above, you put yourself in the category of being a foolish person who has no keys! **Do not let your own traditions make the word of God of no effect!**

(Mark 7:13) Read what God's word says in regards to what we would call foolish: "For *you see your calling, brethren, that not many wise according to the flesh, not many mighty, not many noble, are called. [27]But God has chosen the foolish things of the world to put to shame the wise, and God has chosen the weak things of the world to put to shame the things which are mighty; [28]and the base things of the world and the things which are despised God has chosen, and the things which are not, to bring to nothing the things that are, [29]that no flesh should glory in His presence. [30]But of Him you are in Christ Jesus, who became for us wisdom from God--and righteousness and sanctification and redemption-- [31]that, as it is written, "He who glories, let him glory in the LORD."* (1 Corith 1:26-30).

Here God tells us that many people will not have the benefit of His promises since we do not obey his commands. We have the opportunity to bind our enemies by obeying God. Maybe we should be willing to get out of our traditions which Jesus said would make the word of God of no effect.

I want the word of God to work in my life! Don't you?

12 Gates Into Our Lives

Jerusalem was called the city of peace and had 12 gates. The enemies would try and find a gate that was open to invade and conquer or cause trouble in the city.

God says we are like a city and that we also have 12 gates that we must guard against our enemies gaining entrance, to oppress and destroy us.

In Psalm 24 Our head has 7 gates that we can open and let the Lord of Glory come in. Eyes, nose, ears, and mouth. God wants to come in all seven gates: *[7]Lift up your heads, O you gates! And be lifted up, you everlasting doors! And the King of glory shall come in. [8]Who is this King of glory? The LORD strong and mighty, The LORD mighty in battle. [9]Lift up your heads, O you gates! Lift up, you everlasting doors! And the King of glory shall come n.[0]Who is this King of glory? The LORD of hosts, He is the King of glory. Selah."*

How the Lord comes into our gates

Eyes.

As you read and see the truth; the Lord of Glory is coming in. Creation itself declares the Glory of God.

As Jesus taught the word, he used objects the people could see and get the understanding to the knowledge.

Wives by letting the unsaved husbands "see" their Godly life, can save the husbands. We are living epistles, being read by men! We must become as little children if we want the revelation that takes us deeper into the kingdom of heaven! The apostles not only were seeing the truth, but got to touch and handle the truth! **Jesus was there among them!**

Doubting Thomas not only got to put his finger in the nail-prints of Jesus hands, but was allowed to put his hand up into Jesus side where the Roman soldier thrust his spear! What an awesome experience, but Jesus said we would be more blessed than Thomas if we believed without seeing. **We are blessed!**

Nose.

Two nostrils-- You can smell the Lord (He is called the Rose of Sharon). Many people in their personal times of intimacy with the Lord have smelled that fragrance. He is a real person and has a real fragrance! He says to draw near to Him and He will draw near to us. Let's get close enough to smell Him!

Ears.

As you hear the word of God He is coming in through your two ears. Jesus said to take head what you hear. He also said that he who has ears to hear, let him hear! *"He said My words are spirit and my words are life."* As we hear, we are being spirit filled and life filled! It helps to read the scriptures out loud so the ear gates can hear God's word. As we sing and listen to psalms, and hymns, and spiritual songs the Lord of Glory is coming in. That is why good music edifies and builds us up!

Sex Gate.

Having sex in marriage is a fulfillment of righteousness and is fulfilling and refreshing to the marriage partners. The Lord of Glory comes in through that experience.

God says that sex between marriage partners is a wonderful benefit and each partner is to enjoy the other and is not to withhold that experience from their mate. God says the marriage bed is un-defiled but whoremongers and adulterers, God will judge. Marriage between a man and woman is a covenant, blessed of God!

Feet.

As we let our feet take us to church and out to help and serve others, the Lord says this is a fulfillment of righteousness and you are being filled with Him! We are not to let our feet take us out to do evil. God has ordered our steps and if we walk in His ways, His blessings will pursue us until they overtake us!

God says to be careful to maintain good works till He comes!

WARNING

You can not be saved by good works:

" ^{8} For by grace you have been saved through faith, and that not of yourselves; it is the gift of God, ^{9} not of works, lest anyone should boast."
No one can be justified by good works but needs the blood of Christ to forgive and save them from their sins.

After accepting Jesus Christ as your savior you are suppose to do good works until He comes and He said His rewards will be with Him to reward every man according to his works.. Our works are to bring Glory to our Heavenly Father. **No Work - No Pay!**

Lets get busy so we can all be rewarded and let our works that we do be focused on bringing in the harvest!

The Apostle Paul said we should yield our members (gates) to righteousness and not to sin or corruption.
The same 12 gates we open and let the Lord of Glory come in we can let sin and corruption come in.
In Genesis 4:7 God told Cain that sin was crouched at his door and wanted to get inside Of him. Sin inside of us tries to make us do things we do not want to do, and things we do not allow ourselves to do, and keeps us from doing good things that we should and want to do. (Rom 7:19-20).
Sin is a presence that Satan desires to control us with. God uses personal pronouns to describe sin! God said for us not to give place to the devil. He walks around like a roaring lion seeking whom he may devour. The kingdom that desires to gain entrance into Christians can be summed up in:
"Finally, my brethren, be strong in the Lord and in the power

of His might. *¹¹Put on the whole armor of God that you may be able to stand against the wiles of the devil. ¹²For we do not wrestle against flesh and blood, but against **principalities**, against **powers,** against the **rulers of the darkness of this age, against spiritual hosts of wickedness** in the heavenly places."* (**Ephesians 6:10-12).**

All of our enemies in Satan's kingdom that we wrestle against are in one of those categories.

Satan's kingdom can come into believers as well as unbelievers. In Adam and Eve's transgression, three things gained entrance into human flesh; lust of the eyes, lust of the flesh, and the pride of life.(1st John 2:16).

God made evil for His own purposes. (Prov. 16:4) and everything he made was made to reproduce after its own kind. God made and planted the tree of the knowledge of good and evil in the Garden of Eden. God instructed Adam and told him not to eat from it or he would die.

God did not want man to be like a robot, but gave him a free will so he could love and obey of his own will.

We also show our love to God by obeying him, letting Him rule over us!

In James 1:13-16 *explains how evil is produced in us*

"¹³Let no one say when he is tempted, "I am tempted by God"; for God cannot be tempted by evil, nor does He Himself tempt anyone. ¹⁴But each one is tempted when he is drawn away by his own desires (lust*) and enticed. ¹⁵Then, when desire* (lust*) has conceived, it gives birth to sin; and sin, when it is full-grown, brings forth death.¹⁶Do not be err* (get pregnant and birth evil), *my beloved brethren."*

Here God is telling us that lust in us can get pregnant and produce offspring called sin or corruption. We can give birth to the enemies we are trying to conquer. Let me give you an interesting scripture in Isaiah that will shock you!

*"Behold, the Lord's hand is not shortened, That it cannot save; Nor His ear heavy, That it cannot hear. [2]But your iniquities have separated you from your God; and your sins have hidden His face from you, So that He will not hear. [3]For your hands are defiled with blood, and your fingers with iniquity; Your lips have spoken lies, Your tongue has muttered perversity.[4]No one calls for justice, Nor does any plead for truth. They trust in empty words and speak lies; They **conceive evil** and bring forth* **iniquity**.*[5]They **hatch vipers' eggs** and weave the spider's web; He who **eats of their eggs dies**, And from that which is crushed a* **viper breaks out***.[6]Their webs will not become garments, Nor will they cover themselves with their works;*

*Their works are works of iniquity, And the act of violence is in their hands.[7]Their feet run to evil, And they make haste to shed innocent blood; Their thoughts are thoughts of iniquity; Wasting and destruction are in their paths. [8]The way of peace they have not known, And there is no justice in their ways; They have made themselves crooked paths; Whoever takes that way shall not know peace.[9]Therefore justice is far from us, Nor does righteousness overtake us; We look for light, but there is darkness! For brightness, but we walk in blackness! [10]We grope for the wall like the blind, And we grope as if we had no eyes; We stumble at noonday as at twilight; We are as dead men in desolate places.[11]We all growl like bears, And moan sadly like doves; We look for justice, but there is none; For salvation, but it is far from us.[12]For our transgressions are multiplied before You, And our **sins testify against us***; (out *of our heart proceeds evil thoughts*...thoughts are sins talking to us...

For our transgressions are with us, And as for our iniquities, we know them (Adam knew evil also) *[13]In transgressing and lying against the LORD,*

And departing from our God, Speaking oppression and revolt, **Conceiving** *and uttering from the heart words of falsehood"*. (Isaiah 59:1-13).

Notice what verse 4 says...They conceive evil and bring forth iniquity. The word conceive is the same word as a man and woman coming together in intercourse and the woman's egg *receiving the males sperm and a conception takes place. Verse 5 says **they hatch viper's eggs. That means serpents are being born in us! Shocking isn't it?***

God also says Whoever *"has no rule over his own spirit is like a city broken down, without walls."* (**Prov 25:28**).

Earlier I mentioned the Lord of Glory coming in our 12 gates. It is possible to open and let evil come into us through the same 12 gates!

Remember we can be like a city of peace, if we keep the enemies out.

An important scripture concerning good and evil being able to come into people is very plain in Gal 6:6-10, "⁶Let him who is taught the word share in all good things with him who teaches. ⁷Do not be deceived, God is not mocked; for whatever a man sows, that he will also reap. ⁸For he who sows to his flesh will of the flesh reap corruption, but he who sows to the Spirit will of the Spirit reap everlasting life. ⁹And let us not grow weary while doing good, for in due season we shall reap if we do not lose heart.¹⁰Therefore, as we have opportunity, let us do good to all, especially to those who are of the household of faith."

Here God is saying corruption can come into your flesh if you sow to your flesh! If we as Christians do not believe that, God says we are deceived! We better listen and take heed!

A Christian can sow to his spirit on Sunday morning and sow corruption to his flesh Sunday afternoon. God says that if we do not believe that, we are deceived! If corruption comes in Paul said we would become servants of corruption.

Eyes.

God said to put no evil thing before your eyes. Pornography (corruption) is coming in through people's eyes and they have to serve it! Multitudes of people are in bondage and have become slaves to it. God said if you lust in your heart for (pornography or magazines) after a woman, you are committing adultery with her in your heart. People trapped in pornography over time will end up molesting or raping someone. **Sin can make you do things you hate and would normally not allow yourself to do!**

Violence is also forbidden by God to look at. This is getting into our young people and they are killing their parents, people at school, in the workplace, etc. King David made a covenant with his eyes that he would put no evil thing before his eyes.

Our eyes are the windows of our souls. Better keep your windows closed, or pluck out your right eye.

You can look into people's eyes and see enemies in there. Anger, rage, hatred, murder, depression, fear, etc. We should be seeing peace, joy, and all the fruit of the Holy Spirit in people's eyes and in their countenance.

Ears.

Jesus said to be careful what you hear. He said that words were spirit and His words were life. Evil words such as in rock music talk of death, suicide, depression, rebellion, hatred, failure, filth, etc and will certainly fill you up with spirits of corruption and bondage.We should guard our ears against all filthiness, people speaking doubt and unbelief, and all negative and critical conversations!

I also believe much of the music that has crept into the church is not edifying and is grieving the Holy Spirit. Much of the music is not worship but entertainment! Jesus said His Father wanted people to worship Him in spirit and in truth! Many of the churches sound like the world and it is really hard to tell the difference!

I have ministered to many people who have listened to music with ungodly words and as I commanded the spirits to come out of their ears, they described the pain and tearing feeling as almost unbearable. Many people are losing their hearing that have attended rock music concerts. A lot of that type of music will let in a deaf spirit!

Jesus said to take heed what you hear.

Nose.

People are letting corruption and bondage come in through sniffing cocaine, glue, paint, and all kinds of things to indulge their flesh. Horrible bondages are the result and a life of misery.
Drugs, I guess, are one of the greatest dangers! Multitudes of people have become drug addicts and are in horrible bondage. None of them would have ever believed that they would have ended up an addict!

Satan is a master at bringing people into his bondage. Remember he talked 1/3 of God's angels into following him in his rebellion and their fate was sealed to an everlasting fire prepared for him and the angels! Do not let him talk you into following him. God has a better place for His people. **Jesus said to give no place to the devil.**

Mouth.

The Lord comes in when you confess him as Lord. The scriptures teach that we are eating what we say. Life and death is in the power of the tongue and we are satisfied by the fruit of it!

Be careful what you let in by what you are saying. *"An ungodly witness scorneth judgment: and the mouth of the wicked devoureth iniquity."* (Prov 19:28). When we are saying the wrong things we are eating iniquity and we will be in danger of becoming a worker of iniquity! We are eating life or death. Paul said let all words coming out of our mouth be used for edification and be seasoned with salt. *"But now you yourselves are to put off all these: anger, wrath, malice, blasphemy, filthy language out of your mouth. [9]Do not lie to one another, since you have put off the old man with his deeds."* (Col 3:8-9) Also you should not use your mouth to be a talebearer, gossiper, slanderer, etc.

Of course we can also defile ourselves by giving ourselves too much wine and strong drink. Many people start out in moderation, but God talks about looking on strong drink until a serpent bites them. If you play with a serpent long enough he will bite you!

When you have been bitten, you are in bondage because evil is now in you and will crave wine and strong drink in excess.

Hands.

As you are yielding your hands in doing God's work; the Lord is coming in through those actions.

Even giving someone a glass of water with your hands will someday be rewarded! You use your hands in feeding the hungry and clothing the naked. We will use our hands and all our members either for good or evil.

We can use our hands to hurt people, deal drugs, steal, cheat, murder; make our neighbor drunk (God says a curse comes on us if we do)!

God says if we cannot control our right hand, to cut it off. I had rather control my right hand and use it for good than to cut it off!

Feet

God said if we could not control where our feet want to take us it would be better for us to cut off our right foot than to keep it and our whole body be cast into the lake of fire.

We better get serious about where we allow our feet to take us! Your feet are two gates that evil can enter to wreck havoc in your life. Let's open up our gates and let the Lord of Glory come

Sex Gate.

Sex Gates Are Different From All Others Gates

Outside of marriage having sex is called fornication. Paul said not to do it one time after becoming a Christian, and there are many reasons why we should not:

The Word says, "that *whosoever commit adultery (fornication) is unwise because he destroys his own soul.*" (Prov 6:32).

Your soul will live forever somewhere! What would a man give in exchange for his soul? God asks that question and we need to answer it! If we gain the whole world and all the women in it, and lose or destroy our soul, what would you end up having? A few moments of pleasure and then you will

be in eternity with a destroyed soul, suffering the vengeance of eternal fire prepared for the devil and his angels.

Millions of years, and that would be like a second in eternity. You will have plenty of time to think about how you could have served and witnessed for the Lord and used your members for good instead of evil.

In 1st Corith 10:8 God killed 23,000 of the children of Israel in one day because of that sin and said it was written down as an example for us so we would not tempt God and be dealt with the same way.

God said all sins were without the body except fornication, but that sin is against our own body which is the temple of God.

We actually become one flesh with the person and have an ungodly soul-tie with them. When you have sex outside of marriage you are being defiled with corruption from all their previous sex partners. You get up from the act and leave a part of yourself with the other party.

You are joining Christ to that person in the sexual act. The end result of sexual activity outside of marriage: *"and thou mourn at the last, when thy Flesh and body are consumed."* (Prov 5:11).

People today are trying to find out what causes our flesh and body to be consumed. God tells us one cause for that horrible disease is fornication. *"His own iniquities shall take the wicked himself, and he shall be holden with the cords of his sins."* (Prov 5:22). Why can't we learn from peoples mistakes they have made in the past and are recorded for us? God listed the people's mistakes so we can learn from them.

God even tells us the part of our body that is affected —our liver! (Till a dart strikes through our liver) (Prov 7:23). **Darts are infirmities!**

Prov 7:26 says that a sexually active person has wounded and slain many people! It is like a sexually active person having a legal right to murder people without having to face the authorities and be punished.

There is no such thing as safe sin! A condom can't protect you from evil spirits which will destroy your soul and your body. A survey was conducted several years ago among young girls who had cervical cancer to find out some common characteristics, and one unanimous common similarity was they each had several sexual partners.

God's word says sexual activity outside of marriage causes your flesh and body to be consumed. Are you willing to pay that price to become sexually active?

God says in his word 1st Thes 4:3 "For this is the will of God, even your sanctification that ye should abstain from fornication."

You cannot be sanctified if you are a fornicator because you are allowing corruption to come in to your body and soul!

I read today there is a new thing going on in many colleges called "friends with benefits". This was explained that you can join the movement and your benefits will be you can have sex with any of the friends without any commitment or obligation anytime you desire that pleasure.

God warns us to save ourselves from this evil and adulterous generation! We are to flee fornication...

"His own iniquities shall take the wicked himself, and he shall be holden with the cords of his sins."(Prov 5:22).

Sexual Sins Corrupt Us.

"Lest thou give thine honor to others, and thy years to the cruel." **(Prov 5:9)** *These are evil spirits of corruption that come in to torment and destroy us."* Prov 5:10 lest strangers be filled with thy wealth; and thy labors be in the house of a stranger. The strangers are also spirits that remove your peace and leave guilt and condemnation. Prov 6:31 says the guilty person will lose the contents of his house (life & fruit of the spirit).

Some teaching today says if you catch the thief (Satan) stealing something from you, you can make him return it sevenfold. The scripture they are using is Prov 6:31 where a man is caught in committing adultery and it costs him the contents of his house.

Satan does not restore anything to us but God restores what the palmerworm and cankerworm destroy.

Be encouraged God will forgive you like he did David for his affair with Bathsheba and you can have your soul restored. David said "He restoreth my soul."

After repenting and telling God you are truly sorry, You need to make a decision that you are truly forsaking that sin and plan to never repeat it! After repenting don't say to the other party "see you next week." Tell them it is over forever!

"He that covereth his sins shall not prosper: but whoso confesses and forsakes them shall have mercy.

Confession without forsaking means you get no blood to forgive and cleanse you." (Prov 28:13).

The next step to going free is getting someone to minister to you casting the spirits of corruption out! Remember, corruption is also spirit in nature. God forgives the sin but the corruption needs to be cast out.

I have cast out many spirits of cancer before they started their destructive work. Many times there was a manifestation as the cancer would leave.

Get someone to minister deliverance to you that is not a novice but often deals with evil spirits on a regular basis. Sorry to say many ministers know little or nothing concerning evil spirits, and how they affect God's people. Many of them say that Christians cannot have a demon or an evil spirit. God help us! Christians can have a spirit of fear, deaf spirit, spirit of heaviness, spirit of a broken heart, and the list goes on!

We are perishing for lack of knowledge. Some Ministers today believe in deliverance, however if someone needing deliverance acts up (demon begins to manifest) the person is taken out of the service and away from the very people who need to see and learn by watching the person be delivered from the spirit. Many so called full gospel or charismatic churches are bound by tradition! Jesus would cast the spirits out publicly so everyone could learn by observing.

I was told today of a survey conducted in a major North Carolina University where the students were asked if anyone had ever told them that fornication (sexual activity outside of marriage) was wrong and 90% of the students said no!

What are our parents teaching their children and what are the ministers teaching the parents? We had better return to God's word and work out our own salvation with fear and trembling!

God said that some of the minister's tables are filled with vomit and have caused his people to err because of what they teach. Ministers had better repent and clean up the tables they feed God's sheep from!

Perverted Grace

There is an issue I would like to address in reference to perverted grace teaching…

> " For the grace of God that bringeth salvation hath appeared to all men, teaching us that denying ungodliness and worldly lusts, we should live soberly, righteously, and godly, in this present world; Looking for that blessed hope, and the glorious appearing of the great God and our Savior Jesus Christ. Who gave himself for us, that he might redeem us from all iniquity, and purify unto himself a peculiar people, zealous of good works. "

These things speak, and exhort, and rebuke with all authority. Let no man despise thee.

Titus 2:11 we are being instructed how to live and conduct ourselves that we might be purified from our iniquity and filth and be to God a peculiar people. Christians today want to justify their ungodly lives by saying "I am living under grace, don't put me under condemnation." Grace does not give you a license to commit sin but helps us to be purified. Stop using the scripture to justify yourself by saying, "Where sin abounds grace does much more abound."

When you commit sin ask for the blood of Jesus Christ, which is forgiveness, and you will receive His Grace!

Thank God we are living under Grace!

Warning after Being Delivered!

There are many people today being healed and delivered but few ministers are warning the people concerning the dangers that face people after they have been set free. Read the following account of Jesus healing this man and the warning he gave him!

"After this there was a feast of the Jews, and Jesus went up to Jerusalem. ²*Now there is in Jerusalem by the Sheep Gate a pool, which is called in Hebrew, Bethesda, having five porches.* ³*In*

these lay a great multitude of sick people, blind, lame, paralyzed, waiting for the moving of the water. [4]For an angel went down at a certain time into the pool and stirred up the water; then whoever stepped in first, after the stirring of the water, was made well of whatever disease he had. [5]Now a certain man was there who had an infirmity thirty-eight years. [6]When Jesus saw him lying there, and knew that he already had been in that condition a long time, He said to him, "Do you want to be made well?" [7]The sick man answered Him, "Sir, I have no man to put me into the pool when the water is stirred up; but while I am coming, another steps down before me."[8]Jesus said to him, "Rise, take up your bed and walk." [9]And immediately the man was made well, took up his bed, and walked. And that day was the Sabbath. [10]The Jews therefore said to him who was cured, "It is the Sabbath; it is not lawful for you to carry your bed." [11]He answered them, "He who made me well said to me, "Take up your bed and walk." [12]Then they asked him, "Who is the Man who said to you, "Take up your bed and walk'?" [13]But the one who was healed did not know who it was, for Jesus had withdrawn, a multitude being in that place. [14]Afterward Jesus found him in the temple, and said to him, "See, you have been made well. Sin no more, lest a worse thing come upon you."
(**John 5:1-14**).

Can you imagine a worse thing coming on this man when for 38 years he was unable to get in the water to be healed when the water was stirred by the angel?

In the gospel of Luke Jesus said when the unclean spirit goes out of a man that he will bring 7 more spirits, more wicked than himself and the last state of the man is worse that he was before his deliverance! It is important to repent and turn toward God in the steps He has ordered for us.

Peter's warning.

"If they have escaped the corruption of the world by knowing our Lord and Savior Jesus Christ and are again entangled in it and overcome, they are worse off at the end than they were at the beginning.[21]It would have been better for them not to have

known the way of righteousness, than to have known it and then to turn their backs on the sacred command that was passed on to them. ^{22}*Of them the proverbs are true: "A dog returns to its vomit and, "A sow that is washed goes back to her wallowing in the mud."* **(2 Peter 2:20-22). Remember the devil walks to and fro in the earth seeking whom he may devour! God told Satan he would eat dust the rest of his life. God took dust and made us. Don't be food for the serpent!**

Be healed but be serious about following Jesus Christ!

What You Can Bind On Earth

I have given several examples in scripture and my personal experience about binding things on earth.
Remember things on earth are things you see with your natural earth eyes.

People:
If someone is attempting to harm you in any way you can say to the person, "I bind you in Jesus name according to Matt 18:18). The person will be unable to harm you and many times they will appear as frozen.

People's hands and feet:
If a person's hands are out of control, bind their hands in Jesus name. The same with the feet!

Sea, storm, and wind:
Say what Jesus said "peace be still."

Fire:
"When thou walkest through the fire, thou shall not be burned; neither shall the flame kindle upon thee." (Isaiah 43:2b).

Eyes:
"Be blind for a season."

Animals:
"I bind you in Jesus name."

You Cannot Bind Satan. That will be done by an angel

" *¹ Then I saw an angel coming down from heaven, having the key to the bottomless pit and a great chain in his hand. ²He laid hold of the dragon, that serpent of old, who is the Devil and Satan, and bound him for a thousand years; ³and he cast him into the bottomless pit, and shut him up, and set a seal on him, so that he should deceive the nations no more till the thousand years were finished. But after these things he must be released for a little while."* (**Rev 20:1-3**).

Notice an Angel will do this and not us. Many people today are trying to bind Satan in order to cast out spirits.   Neither Jesus nor any of his disciples ever bound Satan! **Nowhere in scripture did anyone bind Satan to cast out spirits, not even Jesus who had all wisdom and knowledge.**

When Satan is bound (tied up), his works cease on earth until he is loosed again. If the church could bind Satan, why do all the evil works continue to happen in the earth?

Since so many people are constantly binding him, who keeps loosing him?

How Do We Deal With Satan

Satan is in control of the kingdom of darkness and will continue to be until the angel binds him! Satan Is Free To Walk To & Fro In the Earth

In Job 1:6-7 God's word gives us insight into where and what Satan is doing, that we might walk in better understanding of his deceitful, destructive, plan and purpose for our lives. His only desire is to steal, kill, and destroy anyone that is foolish enough to give place to him.

70

His ultimate destination is the lake of fire where he and hell itself will be cast into along with the angels that followed Satan in the rebellion.

You Can Rebuke Him.

To rebuke means to address in a sharp and severe disapproval, reprimand, to force back, check, and sharp reprimand. You can not bind (tie him up)! You also can not send him to hell!

On occasion Jesus rebuked him and also told him to get behind him. Satan uses his forces of evil to do his dirty work.

He bound a woman with a spirit of infirmity 18 years and caused her to walk around bent over and one day Jesus loosed her.

Jesus came to destroy the works of the devil and he gave us the keys to do it! We can learn how to deal with the devil by looking at the temptation experience Jesus encountered in the wilderness, as Satan was tempting him. As we are being tempted we must respond the same way. "Then Jesus was led by the Spirit into the desert to be tempted by the devil. [2]After fasting forty days and forty nights, he was hungry. [3]The tempter came to him and said, If you are the Son of God, tell these stones to become bread [4]Jesus answered, it is written: 'Man does not live on bread alone, but on every word that comes from the mouth of God [5]Then the devil took him to the holy city and had him stand on the highest point of the temple. [6] If you are the Son of God, he said throw yourself down. For it is written: He will command his angels concerning you, and they will lift you up in their hands, so that you will not strike your foot against a stone. [7]Jesus answered him, It is also written: Do not put the Lord your God to the test. [8]Again, the devil took him to a very high mountain and showed him all the kingdoms of the world and their splendor. [9] All this I will give you," he said, if you will bow down and worship me. [10]Jesus said to him, Away from me, Satan! For it is written: 'Worship the Lord your God, and serve him only. [11]Then the devil left him and

angels came and attended him." (Matt 4:1-11).

Notice that Jesus spoke the word of God back to Satan with each temptation. Jesus did not bind him, send him to hell or the pit, or any other crazy thing like the body of Christ is doing today in their so called spiritual warfare. Jesus sets the example for us to follow.

The Lord told me one time that I could not improve on the way he did things and for me not to try! We are to be imitators of Christ. We must know the word if we are to resist the devil with the word when we are tempted.

I would like to share an experience I had when Satan tempted me one day in Morehead City, NC. I had been making calls, presenting a retirement plan to beauty shops in many NC cities. Many of these beauty shops had several employees. I told everyone in there that I wanted to tell them about a miracle God did in my life. Everyone was open to hear about my miracle so I had a captive audience. I shared that I was born with a one inch short leg and had to wear a lift in my shoe to build up that leg. As a result of the short leg my lower back would cause me to have a lot of pain at times. I had been to Chiropractors for help many times, but the help would only be temporary. My brother Owen Johnson, who is a minister of the gospel, came by my insurance office one day and said he would like to pray that God would heal me. I had been raised in a denominational church and had never seen anyone instantly healed of anything, especially a short leg and back trouble. Never had I seen a blind, deaf and dumb, lame, or any type of demoniac healed in any of the church services. He said before praying for me that he wanted to share two scriptures with me. *"Jesus Christ the same yesterday, and today, and forever."* (Heb 13:8).

The same Jesus that walked this earth almost 2,000 years ago doing all the wonderful miracles, healings, signs, and wonders, is the same today. The only difference is you can not see him now except by faith. By faith we must believe he has been raised from the dead and is alive and seated in heaven at his Fathers right hand, waiting for people to pray asking him to do the same works today! We should also be able by faith to see Christ in each other and working through each other.

Jesus Christ, if He is formed in us, is the same as He was walking the earth nearly 2,000 years ago. We are living by His faith doing the works that He did when He was walking outside of us!

Jesus Christ is the same whether He is inside or outside of your body! He wants to do the same works today, but needs you to do them through. Paul instructs us to minister according to the power that works within us. The other scripture he shared became one of my favorites! "*Verily, verily, I say unto you, He that believeth on me, the works that I do shall he do also; and greater works than these shall he do; because I go unto my Father. And whatsoever ye shall ask in my name, that will I do, that the* Father might be glorified in the Son. If ye shall ask anything in my name, I will do it."

After sharing these **two scriptures he asked me if I would give God the glory if he grew out my short leg and healed my back. I told my brother I would since I knew he could not do it without God working through him.**

Nicodemus told Jesus he knew that God was with him because he could not do the things he did unless God was with him.

Sitting in a chair with my legs fully stretched out and extended in front of me he asked Jesus to heal me and immediately it was as if something hot was poured on my short leg and bad back and within five seconds my leg had grown equal to the other. I saw it as it grew out!

That experience caused me to surrender to God's calling and I have never looked back! After sharing this testimony with the people I would ask if anyone present had a short leg or back trouble. In every beauty shop either the operators or customers would acknowledge their need for a miracle. All the people would gather around to watch like players in a football huddle. God would grow out their short legs and heal their back problems.

After seeing God's power demonstrated, most of the people present would accept Christ or re-dedicate their lives as the Holy Spirit would convict and draw them. Many were being filled with the Holy Spirit and delivered from their torments and oppression. God was using me in the highways and hedges! That is where the harvest fields are and we must go outside of the church walls if we plan to bring in the harvest of lost souls. This was happening several times a day as I worked my way from city to city toward Morehead City where my day would end.

Satan Tempts Me

After a wonderful seafood dinner, as I was leaving the restaurant, I observed a very wealthy looking man sitting on a bench in front of the restaurant. He had the gold chains, diamonds, and everything about him looked like wealth. I sat down on the bench with him and asked if he went to church. Immediately his head slumped forward on the cane in his right hand as though he had fainted. Out of his mouth came these words, "if you will stop doing what you are doing, I will give you anything you want, money, gold, houses, land, women, and even a church." As I listened to those words, I was shocked almost beyond belief. This man did not know me and I had never seen him. I knew exactly what that voice meant when it said I will give you anything if you will stop doing what you are doing. That day I had been making a difference in influencing people to follow Jesus Christ. Satan was offering me a deal as he had offered Jesus certain things if he would obey him.

I responded by saying, "what did you say?" The same offer was repeated as his head remained slumped resting on the cane. This left me weak and stunned as my flesh wanted everything the voice had offered.

I must have sat there pondering what had just happened to me for at least a minute and finally I was able to utter "I am going to serve the Lord Jesus Christ all the days of my life and I will never stop serving him."

Instantly the man raised his head and acted like he had just awakened out of sleep. He stood up and very politely said "good day," as he walked away. I had dealt with Satan by resisting him with the words I spoke to him!

In the book of Job, Satan told God that he could make Job curse Him if given permission to afflict him. God gave him permission but would not allow Satan to kill him.

Later in the book of Job after Satan had literally wiped out Job and his possessions, Satan spoke those very words through Job's wife, "why don't you curse God and die." Satan was also speaking through Peter when Jesus answered Peter by looking at him and saying "get behind me Satan." Many times Satan talks to us today through people who are speaking things contrary to God's word, his principals and his plan and purposes for our lives.

Submit yourself to God, resist the devil and he will flee from you! Resist him with *it is written.*

A brother in Christ recently shared a testimony with me concerning Satan appearing to him and offering to give him his hearts desire if he would worship and serve him, and obey his instructions. Satan showed him a long narrow building several hundred miles long that was filled with everything he could ever want. Motorcycles, cars, houses, Rolex watches, women, and anything his heart could ever imagine.

He agreed to serve him and his first instructions were for him to go to a certain minister's home where he had attended church in years past. He appeared on the ministers steps about midnight and as the surprised minister asked why he was there at such a late hour he responded, "I have come here to kill you."

He said the next thing he remembered was waking up with many Christians surrounding and praying for him. He said he felt like he was on fire because of the presence of God that came in the room.They were casting spirits out of him that entered when he had yielded to Satan and his kingdom of darkness.

There are churches today called the church of Satan or Wicca churches. Some of these are available on our military bases as they are tax exempt like any other church. Many people today, who have killed others, make the statement that a voice told them to do it. Satan has come to steal, kill, and destroy, and he uses people to do his will and purposes. In Galatians 5:19-21. The works of Satan are the works of the flesh and one of these is murder.

The works of the flesh are a big part of what Jesus came to destroy that we might be more like him!

"The acts of the sinful nature are obvious: sexual immorality, impurity and debauchery; [20]*idolatry and witchcraft; hatred, discord, jealousy, fits of rage, selfish ambition, factions* [21] *and envy; drunkenness, , dissensions, orgies, and the like. I warn you, as I did before, that those who live like this will not inherit the kingdom of God."* (Gal 6:19 -21).

Jesus Christ became all these sins that we could be delivered from every one of them! We are justified from *them* when we are born again and then we are to lay aside the sins one by one and God will cleanse us as we *confess* and forsake them! We can be an over-comer since Jesus overcame!

A person when he is born- again does not get rid of all his sins at that time but is justified (just as though he had never sinned). He still must lay aside (put off), our sins after the salvation experience to become sanctified.

How Satan Talks to Us

Satan is talking to us many times each day through thoughts that are speaking to us out of our heart. Jesus said out of our heart proceed evil thoughts. In Ecclesiastes 10:20b these thoughts are called a voices It is Satan's voice trying to get you to commit the works of the flesh.

" *[19]For out of the heart proceed evil thoughts, murders, adulteries, fornications, thefts, false witness, and blasphemies. [20]These are the things which defile a man, but to eat with unwashed hands does not defile a man."* (Matt 15:19-20). Look at what else Jesus says comes out of our heart He said to them, *"Are you thus without understanding also? Do you not perceive that whatever enters a man from outside cannot defile him, [19]because it does not enter his heart but his stomach, and is eliminated, thus purifying all foods?" [20]And He said, "What comes out of a man that defiles a man. [21]For from within, out of the heart of men, proceed evil thoughts, adulteries, fornications, murders, [22]thefts, covetousness, wickedness, deceit, lewdness, an evil eye, blasphemy, pride, foolishness. [23]All these evil things come from within and defile a man "(Mark 7:18-23).* If we would do what Satan is tempting us to do with these thoughts (voices) coming out of our heart, we would truly be a worker of iniquity serving the devil! Jesus came to destroy these works of the devil! He tells us how to deal with this. *"[3]For though we walk in the flesh, we do not war according to the flesh. [4]For the weapons of our warfare are not carnal but mighty in God for pulling down strongholds, [5]casting down arguments and every high thing that exalts itself against the knowledge of God, bringing every thought into captivity to the obedience of Christ, [6]and being ready to punish all disobedience when your obedience is fulfilled."(2 Corith 10:3-6).*

Remember every thought you have has a source and the source is sin or corruption that is talking to you out of your heart. When you capture the thought, determine who is talking to you. It could be God talking to you through the word that has been hidden in your heart. If God is talking to you he will not be telling you to disobey his commandments and principals laid out in his word. Remember how the word in you will teach, lead, and keep you!

" *20My son, keep your father's commandment, and do not forsake the law of your mother. Bind them continually upon thine heart, and tie them about thy neck; 22When you roam, they will lead you; when you sleep, they will keep you; and when you awake, they will speak with you.*" (Prov 6:20-22).

After determining it is the enemy trying to lead you into unrighteousness, tell God that you want to be free from the enemy in your heart that is speaking. If the thoughts are to commit adultery, confess adultery as a sin and the blood of Jesus will cleanse you. Whatever area of disobedience it is suggesting; confess it as sin and again the blood of Jesus will cleanse you. Paul said to lay aside the sin (voice) that so easily besets you God said blessed are the pure in heart as they shall see (hear) God.

Can you imagine not having any evil thoughts and only having God's thoughts coming out of your heart to lead and guide you continually! So Satan can talk to us out of our heart, through another person, or like he did to Jesus. In person!

Danger of Conversing With Evil Spirits

We know Satan is known as the deceiver and his plan is to deceive us into believing a lie. When a person is dealing with spirits in a person and they manifest by speaking through the person, it is easy to be drawn into a conversation with them as they desire to mislead and guide you into error. Many times the demons want to give you so called "privileged information" to get you lifted up in pride and carry you away from the truth.

Some Christians try to justify their actions by quoting the case in Mark 5:9 where Jesus asked the spirit his name. Jesus had already commanded the spirit to come out and he addresses it as an un-clean spirit. When the spirit began to talk to Jesus then

Jesus asked him his name. A spirit named Legion identified itself and said there were many spirits inside of the man. All of the spirits began to talk through the man, begging Jesus to allow them permission to enter the swine. The only dialogue in Jesus response was "go".

Some people ministering deliverance and conversing with the spirits use as an excuse that if you capture a natural enemy you have the right to interrogate him by asking all kinds of questions.

The scriptures tell us that Satan is a liar, and the father of lies, and there is no truth in him. Demons or evil spirits will speak those lies to you trying to convince you to believe a lie, thus deceiving you. Do not be drawn into Satan's trap designed to get you to listen to half truths which are a lie! These lies pertaining to deliverance will end up making you in-effective and you will be responsible for causing other believers to depart from sound doctrine. There is a warning in scripture that teachers will receive a greater judgment and punishment. Just prove things out with scripture before you teach what others are sharing.

Jesus forbade us from seeking out people with familiar spirits to obtain knowledge and spiritual understanding. The penalty for doing this was death to both parties. Very serious consequences for disobedience!

We as Christians have the Holy Spirit with all the gifts, including the gift of discerning of spirits to reveal things to us, so why would we want to ask Satan or his demons for information concerning setting a person free?

Jesus said a kingdom divided against itself will not stand and I can assure you, that neither Satan nor his wicked spirits are anxious to be cast into their final destination, the lake of fire, where they will be tormented day and night, forever and ever! One day a demon, speaking through a man asked Jesus if He had come to torment him before his time. They know their time is coming and will do everything possible to delay that event!

The Lord told me one day as I was studying His word that I could not improve on the way He did things, and for me to do things the way He did them. We are to be imitators of Christ.

When Jesus ministered to people oppressed with evil spirits, He either cast the spirits out, or loosed the people from the spirits.

Can Satan Read your Mind?

Many people want to know if Satan can read our mind or tell what we are thinking.

By the evil thoughts Jesus said that come out of our heart, Satan and his spirits are the ones talking to us. Through dreams and visions they can also communicate out of our heart. They certainly know what they are communicating to us. Their plan is to deceive, torment and mislead God's people.

I am not sure if they know what God is communicating to us out of our heart. If they do know I am sure they would try to put doubt and unbelief in our minds to keep us from acting on God's word He would be speaking to us...

Every wind of doctrine is blowing to deceive, lead astray, and destroy Christians, so be careful to prove all things, and hold fast to that which is good!

How to Turn Away Wrath

God in His word gives us all His wisdom, knowledge, and understanding to every problem and situation we could ever face now or in the future.

One of the enemies we will face in the perilous times we are now living in is the spirit of wrath (one of the works of the flesh in Gal 6:20). Wrath working through people can be very dangerous and destructive and we will need to use our spiritual weapons to protect ourselves and others. God says my people perish for lack of knowledge therefore we must know and apply His knowledge in our everyday lives. *"A soft answer turns away wrath: but grievous words stir up anger."* The word of God is like a two edge sword so when you answer a person or situation with a soft answer, you are sticking your sword into the situation to silence your enemy. Your sword will always conquer your enemies. Your sword is God!

I would like to share an experience where this principal worked for me in an amazing way.

I was very busy one day doing God's work and as I was

driving my car and making calls in a small community with secondary roads, I would slow down trying to find the address of a place I was going to visit. This large 18 wheeler truck was behind me and kept persistently blowing his air-horn behind me not knowing what to do, I pulled into a parking lot off the road so he could pass me.

The truck driver pulled in behind me and jumped out of his truck and as he approached my car, I could see he had a black-jack swinging violently in his hand as he walked up to the window of my car which I had rolled halfway down. His face was contorted with the rage that was manifesting and he was swearing all kinds of profanity as he raised the black-jack to strike me through the open window. The scripture came up in my spirit *"a soft answer turns away wrath."*

God was handing me a sword to defend myself! My soft answer was "I am sorry if I offended you by having to slow down looking for an address." "I am sorry." Immediately his countenance changed and he stomped away muttering to himself

Another alternative would have been to say "I bind you in the name of Jesus Christ,." And the angel of the Lord would have held him for me! Thank God the weapons of our warfare are mighty, through God, to the pulling down of strong-holds!

Use your sword (soft answer) to turn away wrath in your home, and wherever you might be when the rage sticks up its ugly head!

God told me a sign that would be very obvious to His people that the end was near, would be a manifesting of **rage (wrath)** in the lives of people. Are we not seeing it increase in people such as "road rage" husband and wife abuse, children killing each other, parents killing their children, ethnic group rage, etc? The scripture the Lord gave me was *"therefore rejoice ye heavens and ye that dwell in them. Woe to the inhabiters of the earth and the sea! For the devil is come down unto you, having great wrath; because he knoweth that he hath but a short time."(Rev:12:12).*

Wrath is one of the works of the flesh mentioned in Gal 5:19. Do not let wrath in you as the devil will use you to express his wrath! Wrath is part of the "root of bitterness" mentioned in Heb 12:15 and it comes in through resentment and unforgiveness! **Keep that root out as it will trouble you and others if it gets established.**

Jesus Said To Loose People By Remitting Their Sins.

How to Remit Sin

Webster's new world dictionary says to remit means forgive or pardon (sins), to refrain from inflicting punishment, to cancel **That's what Jesus commanded us to teach and preach.**

A good example of this is when Stephen was being stoned to death. Read the account below.

"And he kneeled down, and cried with a loud voice, Lord; lay not this sin to their charge. And when he had said this, he fell asleep. This ultimately would have probably cost them their life."

Webster's definition says Stephen cancelled their debt, pardoned them, and caused God to refrain from inflicting punishment on them.

Read the entire account: *"[57]Then they cried out with a loud voice, stopped their ears, and ran at him with one accord; [58]and they cast him out of the city and stoned him. And the witnesses laid down their clothes at the feet of a young man named Saul. [59]And they stoned Stephen as he was calling on God and saying, "Lord Jesus, receive my spirit." [60]Then he knelt down and cried out with a loud voice, "Lord, do not charge them with this sin." And when he had said this, he fell asleep."*

Jesus Remitted Sins

As they were crucifying Jesus, he remitted their sins.

Read His very words: " *[34]Then Jesus said, "Father, forgive them, for they do not know what they do."*
Can you imagine the judgment he prevented from coming on the ones who crucified him?

He pardoned the people and we can also pardon and cancel people's sins preventing God's judgment from coming on them.

We are told to preach repentance and remission of sins to all nations. " *[47]And that repentance and remission of sins should be preached in his name among all nations" (,* Luke 24:47).

"If you forgive the sins of any, they are forgiven them; if you retain the sins of any, they are retained." (John 20:23)
We have the authority to determine whether a person is pardoned or punished. We had better show people mercy so we might receive mercy.

Jesus not only remitted and pardoned people, he said we could also. The following incident shows Jesus remitting a man's sin.
" *[1] And again He entered Capernaum after some days, and it was heard that He was in the house. [2]Immediately many gathered together, so that there was no longer room to receive them, not even near the door. And He preached the word to them. [3]Then they came to Him, bringing a paralytic who was carried by four men. [4]And when they could not come near Him because of the crowd, they uncovered the roof where He was. So when they had broken through, they let down the bed on which the paralytic was lying.*

[5]When Jesus saw their faith, He said to the paralytic, **"Son, your sins are forgiven you."** *[6]And some of the scribes were sitting there and reasoning in their hearts, [7]"Why does this Man*

*speak blasphemies like this? **Who can forgive sins but God
alone?"***

*[8]But immediately, when Jesus perceived in His spirit that they
reasoned thus within themselves, He said to them, "Why do you
reason about these things in your hearts? [9]Which is easier, to
say to the paralytic, "Your sins are forgiven you,' or to say,
"Arise, take up your bed and walk'? [10]But that you may know
that the Son of Man has power on earth to forgive sins"--He said
to the paralytic, [11]"I say to you, arise, take up your bed, and go
to your house." [12]Immediately he arose, took up the bed, and
went out in the presence of them all, so that all were amazed and
glorified God, saying, "We never saw anything like this!"*

**The people were upset with Jesus for pardoning the man's
sins. People today may question Christian's right to forgive
and pardon people for their sins.**

**The people will still have to confess and forsake their sins
to go free from their bondage; however you by remitting
their sins are withholding God's judgment from affecting
them.**

**What a difference it would make if we remitted each others
sins in the home…Husbands, wives, and children sending
away each others sins! Look how the church could become
healthier it we remitted sins instead of judging and
condemning each other!**

Repentance and Water Baptism to Remit Sins

In Luke 3:3 and he went into all the region around the Jordan,
preaching a baptism of repentance for the remission of sins,

Here John the Baptist was preaching to all the crowds that
came to be baptized of him in water that they should repent of all
their sins, for the remission of their sins. It is important to be
baptized in water after becoming a believer in Jesus Christ. Most

people call this being born-again or being born from above by God's spirit.

When you are baptized in water your sins are washed away. (Remitted)...sent away!

Read this in Acts 22:14-16 [4] *"Then he said: 'The God of our fathers has chosen you to know his will and to see the Righteous One and to hear words from his mouth.* [15] *You will be his witness to all men of what you have seen and heard.* [16] *And now what are you waiting for? Get up, be baptized and* **<u>wash your sins away</u>**, *(calling on his name)."*

Remember sin in the flesh of a believer will try to make him do things he hates and does not allow himself to do; and will try to prevent him from doing the good things he wants to do. Paul said in his flesh dwelt no good thing.

God forgives you when you ask but **<u>He washes them away</u>** when you are **<u>baptized in water.</u>** Jesus was our example as John the Baptist baptized him (submerged him) in water.

The children of Israel as they were passing through the Red sea, is an example of our enemies being washed away. Pharaoh and all his men were drowned (washed away)

Have someone baptize you in water if you have not already done so! The thief on the cross was not able to have his sins washed away with water baptism, but it did not prevent him from going to paradise with Jesus that day because he was forgiven (justified). We are washed with the water of the word as we are obedient to the word. Jesus gave us the word to be baptized!

You Cannot Cast Out Sin

Many people ministering deliverance today are trying to cast out sins instead of evil spirits and thus there is much confusion concerning what is an evil spirit that can be cast out of a person.

If you ask people today what sin is, most would say it is missing the mark or falling short of the glory of God. That is not a good definition of sin. Sin is a **presence that can cause you to miss the mark or to fall short of the glory of God.** Let's look at how God was talking about sin being a presence. God was talking to Cain concerning the sacrifice he had offered him and here God gives us great insight concerning sin and what it can cause you to do if it gains access into your life.

"And the LORD said unto Cain, Why art thou wroth? And why is thy countenance fallen? [7]If thou doest well, shalt thou not be accepted? And if thou doest not well, sin lieth at the door. And unto thee shall be his desire, and thou shalt rule over him." (Genesis 4: 6-7). Here God is describing sin by using personal pronouns to describe him like it was a person. Cain did not do well and let sin in his door and sin manifested as one of works of the flesh called murder. Cain murdered his brother Abel! Sin has power and abilities that can influence and force you to serve it. Reckon yourself dead to sin and alive to righteousness! *"Now the works of the flesh are evident, which are: adultery, fornication, uncleanness, lewdness, [20]idolatry, sorcery, hatred, contentions, jealousies, outbursts of wrath, selfish ambitions, dissensions, heresies, [21]envy, murders, drunkenness, revelries, and the like; of which I tell you beforehand, just as I also told you in time past, that those who practice such things will not inherit the kingdom of God." (Gal 6:19-21).* There are 18 works of the flesh listed here and if we do not do well as God told Cain, sin can enter and make us do any number of these things that we hate and do not allow ourselves to do. Sin has a personality and a desire and that is to rule over you! Paul said he who commits sin is the servant of sin! To make this easy to understand, since sin has a personality lets say that several people are trying to get in your

house (life) to cause you to serve them. Let's name them Steve, Bill, Barbara, and Susan

Steve: His personality is sexual sins. If you let him in your life, he will do his best to get you to commit Adultery. This is what he enjoys and thinks about constantly and will do anything to persuade or entice you into that sin and cause you to break God's commandment. (Thou shall not commit adultery). If you are now committing Adultery you are in bondage and are serving Steve.

Bill: He likes to hate certain people and will do his best to use you in being cruel and harsh and unkind. He will do his best to keep you from showing love and compassion to people. Are you serving Bill? If so you are in bondage to him!

Barbara: She likes to get drunk and party. She looks forward to the weekends so she can manifest the works of the flesh called drunkenness. And reveling. She loves the wild nightlife and enjoys seducing many people who love to party with her. Are you in bondage to Barbara?

Susan: She loves witchcraft and anything to do with the occult or any kind of spiritism. She loves to read occult books such as Harry Potter and books on Sorcery and how to put curses on people. She is so hungry for the occult and will stand in line all night when a new edition of Harry Potter is released.

How to Go Free

God made a way for us to go free from being a slave to sin (Steve, Bill, Barbara, and Susan.)

Jesus Christ became sin for us and gave us his blood to cleanse us, and set us free from the yoke of bondage to sin!

We Must Hate Sin (Steve, Bill, Barbara, and Susan) and desire to forever forsake them, cutting all ties and connections. Never go where they may be hanging out.

The scriptures say it this way. *"He who covers his sins will not prosper, but whoever* **confesses and forsakes** *them will have mercy." (*Prov. 28:13).

The mercy is the blood of Jesus Christ and forgiveness of our sins making us justified before God.

Paul describes sin and its ability and desire, *"For we know that the law is spiritual, but I am carnal, sold under sin. [15]For what I am doing, I do not understand. For what I will to do, that I do not practice; but what I hate, that I do. [16]If, then, I do what I will not to do, I agree with the law that it is good. [17]But now, it is no longer I who do it, but sin that dwells in me. [18]For I know that in me (that is, in my flesh) nothing good dwells; for to will is present with me, but how to perform what is good I do not find. [19]For the good that I will to do, I do not do; but the evil I will not to do, that I practice. [20]Now if I do what I will not to do, it is no longer I who do it, but sin that dwells in me."(Romans 7:14-20).*

When we are born-again, we have tasted the heavenly gift (the spirit of Christ) and have received a new spirit, and have the desire to serve and please the Lord Jesus Christ. The sin and corruption in our flesh that Paul describes, is at war with the spirit of Christ in us. The sin in us does not want us to obey God thus opposes our walk of obedience in Him. The Apostle Paul tells us to lay aside that sin that so easily besets us. *"Therefore we also, since we are surrounded by so great a cloud of witnesses, let us lay aside every weight, and the sin which so easily ensnares us, and let us run with endurance the race that is set before us, [2]looking unto Jesus, the author and finisher of our faith, who for the joy that was set before Him endured the cross, despising the shame, and has sat down at the right hand of the throne of God. For consider Him who endured such hostility from sinners against Himself, lest you become weary and discouraged in your souls. [4]You have not yet resisted to bloodshed,* **striving against sin"** *(Heb 12:1-4).*

If you were waist deep sinking in quick-sand, would you strive against the problem with all your heart and strength, willing to do anything to save yourself from death?

God has given you a way of escape so call on Jesus now to

have mercy and deliver you from your sin or bondage. Confess and be willing to forsake it now and live the abundant life he has for you! (Prov 16:6)

⁶By mercy and truth iniquity is purged: and by the fear of the LORD men depart from evil. Depart from Bill, Steve, Barbara, and Susan (all your sins). Remember God will not separate you from your friends but only who you consider to be your enemies.

"THOU HAST LOVED RIGHTEOUSNESS, AND HATED INIQUITY; THEREFORE GOD, EVEN THY GOD, HATH ANOINTED THEE WITH THE OIL OF GLADNESS ABOVE THY FELLOWS" (Heb 1:9)

We Must Hate Sin to be Free

<u>Paul lists a number of the sins we face today</u>

"Do you not know that the unrighteous will not inherit the kingdom of God? Do not be deceived. Neither fornicators, nor idolaters, nor adulterers, nor homosexuals, nor sodomites, nor thieves, nor covetous, nor drunkards, nor revilers, nor extortioners will inherit the kingdom of God. And such were some of you. But you were washed, but you were sanctified, but you were justified in the name of the Lord Jesus, and by the Spirit of our God." (1ˢᵗ Corith 6:9-11).

Paul was writing this to Christians who were already born again, and he was explaining the process of going free from their sins and corruption. The process included deliverance from evil spirits.

Paul said to lay aside that sin that so easily besets us. When we acknowledge our sin and confess it to God, we are justified, just as though we had never sinned.

The next step in the process is to be washed with the water of the word. As you hear and meditate on the word you are being cleansed with the water that came out of our Lord Jesus Christ. (He came to us by water and blood).

The final step is to be sanctified. This includes deliverance from the spirits of corruption and defilement that came in through our transgressions. (Sin in us causes us to transgress God's Laws).

Paul said some of the Christians had been guilty of the sins listed above including homosexuality. God loves the homosexual, the adulterers, the drunkards as well as the murderers, and here Paul is telling them the process to not only be forgiven, but to be washed and cleaned!

People in bondage to any of the sins listed can know there is hope for complete and total victory!

First a person must agree with God when He calls something a sin or an abomination. You can not call your sin an alternate lifestyle and go free. With that deception a murderer would also say it was an alternate life-style. So would a thief, and so would a liar. We must let God's word show us what is good or evil and then come into agreement with Him.

Many homosexuals and lesbians today are trying to go free from their bondages to sin. Be encouraged - It is called the 3 step program:

• Be Justified (calling on Jesus Christ to forgive and save you from your sins).

• Be Washed (God is washing His bride with the water of the word). Obedience to His word washes you!

• Be Sanctified (the process of being saved & delivered).

Who the son sets free is free indeed!

I have just shared one of the laws in Romans chapter 7 called the law of sin and death.

The law of the spirit of life in Christ Jesus will deliver you from the law of sin and death. The more of Christ that is formed in you after being born again, (Gal 4:19) the more you are being delivered from the law of sin and death! When Christ is fully formed in you, you would be totally free with no condemnation! (Rom 8:1).

We are being saved which is a process that begins with the new birth! We are being born-again as the process continues!

You also would be called a son of God, not a babe, or teenage son...*Gal 4:6-7" and because you are sons, God has sent forth the Spirit of His Son into your hearts, crying out, "Abba, Father!" Therefore you are no longer a slave but a son, and if a son, then an heir of God through Christ. Those who are led by the spirit of God are sons of God!" (Matt 5:25-26).*

Agree With Your Adversary (Satan) Quickly!

Until Christ has been formed completely in us, God has made a way for us to walk free without guilt and condemnation.

"Agree with your adversary quickly, while you are on the way with him, lest your adversary deliver you to the judge, the judge hand you over to the officer and you be thrown into prison. Assuredly, I say to you, you will by no means get out of there till you have paid the last penny." (Matt 5:25-26).

Many Christians are walking around today with guilt and condemnation because of sins they have committed. They will not agree with their accuser, the devil, that they have missed the mark and so he has a legal right to accuse and torment them.

To go free tell Satan that you did sin, but you are going to confess the sin, and the blood of Jesus Christ is going to cleanse you and set you free so he will not be able to condemn you for that mistake.

When we sin we must be quick to ask God for forgiveness so we will not have anything Satan can use to condemn us for! Glory!

Thank God for 1st John 1:9 if we confess our sins, he is faithful and just to forgive us our sins, and to cleanse us from all unrighteousness.

*"Do you not know that to whom you present yourselves slaves to obey, you are that one's slaves whom you obey, whether of sin leading to death, or of obedience leading to righteousness? But God be thanked that though you were slaves of sin, yet you obeyed from the heart that form of doctrine to which you were delivered. And having been set free from sin, you became slaves of righteousness. I speak in human terms because of the weakness of your flesh. For just as you presented your members as slaves of uncleanness, and of lawlessness leading to more lawlessness, so now present your members as **slaves of righteousness** unto **holiness.** For when you were slaves of sin, you were free in regard to righteousness. What fruit did you have then in the things of which you are now ashamed? For the end of those things is death. But now having been set free from sin, and having become slaves of God, you have your fruit to holiness, and the end, everlasting life. For the wages of sin is death, but the gift of God is eternal life in Christ Jesus our Lord."(Rom 6:16-23).*

As previously we used human names to bring simple clear understanding to sin being a personality; now let's use names to represent righteousness that comes through obedience to the word of God.

"My son, keep my words, And treasure my commands within you. Keep my commands and live, and my law as the apple of your eye. Bind them on your fingers; Write them on the tablet of your heart. Say to wisdom, "You are my sister," And call

understanding your nearest kin that they may keep you from the immoral woman, from the seductress who flatters with her words."(Prov 7:1-5).

Here God is calling the word of God our sister and understanding our kinswoman. If we get our sister and kinswoman inside of us they can talk to us saying not to be involved with the seductress, allowing the law of sin and death to put us in bondage.

Imagine having many of God's children (the word of God) inside of us and them directing our steps. David said," I hide your word in my heart that I will not sin against you."

Psalm 119:105 "Thy word is a lamp unto my feet, and a light unto my path. We are walking in darkness if we are not walking in the light (word)." **BE CAREFUL WHERE YOU STEP!**

My son, keep your father's command, And do not forsake the law of your mother. Bind them continually upon your heart; Tie them around your neck. When you roam, they will lead you; when you sleep, they will keep you; and when you awake, they will speak with you. GOD inside of us can lead us as we go, keep us when we sleep, and talk to us when we are awake. God says my sheep hear my voice (speaking from within us) and through his preachers and teachers. Jesus said if they receive you, they receive me.

In the beginning was the word, and the word was with God, and the word was God. The word is still God and will always be God! Heaven and earth will pass away but his word will never pass away. God in us will be forever because our body is the temple of God, the Holy Spirit, and Jesus Christ. God calls this a mystery that has been hidden but is now being revealed!

Why Binding and Loosing works

The keys to the kingdom of God work because Jesus himself said, I have the keys to death, hell, and the grave. God has given

Jesus Christ, his son, a name above every name, that everyone in heaven and earth must bow their knee to his name (keys) when used! We are all subject to that name. Satan and devils are terrified of that name. Someday even they will have to bow their knee in front of Jesus Christ and confess that Jesus Christ is Lord!

We must hide the word in our heart that we may know and hear His voice and remember his commandments to do them! Jesus said if a man loves me he will keep my words: and my Father and I will come unto him and we will make our abode with him.

Wow, the Father and His Son coming to live inside of us! That truly is a hidden mystery. The world would never believe that God, the Father and His Son, Jesus Christ, live inside of the believers on earth.

" ¹⁶And what agreement has the temple of God with idols? For you are the temple of the living God. As God has said: I will dwell in them and walk among them. I will be their God, And they shall be My people." Think of God, the Father and Jesus Christ walking inside of us to and fro in the earth reconciling man back to Himself.

Let's hurry and get Christ "formed" in us so we can have the Father formed in us also! John 17:3 "and this is eternal life that they may know you, the only true God, and Jesus Christ whom you have sent." What wonderful fellowship we would have with them on this earth—It would truly be like having Heaven on Earth. That is a mystery indeed!

"Jesus Master Card"

Think of the name of Jesus Christ as a major credit card backed by all of heaven. His name is good anywhere and in Him there is no limit to those who believe!

They Needed the "MasterCard."

From the following incident in the scriptures you can see that we will need the keys at times to protect ourselves and others. *"Then some of the itinerant Jewish exorcists took it upon themselves to call the name of the Lord Jesus over those who had evil spirits, saying, "We exorcise you by the Jesus whom Paul preaches."* [14]*Also there were seven sons of Sceva, a Jewish chief priest, who did so.* [15]*And the evil spirit answered and said, "Jesus I know, and Paul I know; but who are you?"* [16]*Then the man in whom the evil spirit was leaped on them, overpowered them, and prevailed against them, so that they fled out of that house naked and wounded.* [17]*This became known both to all Jews and Greeks dwelling in Ephesus; and fear fell on them all, and the name of the Lord Jesus was magnified."*(*Acts 19:13-17).*

Imagine someone strong enough to undress and wound a priests seven sons!

Remember if you bind the person (strong man) the spirits within him can not use him to take off your clothes and wound you!

What You Can Loose On Earth

Husbands
Wives
Children
Churches
Pastors
People from sickness, diseases, infirmities, bondages, etc.
Cities & Nations
Creation itself
Ministers in prison (like Peter).

In Isaiah it says when Zion travails she brings forth her children. I believe the keys will work in our prayer and intercession also. Let me give a model prayer using the keys.

To Loose Children

Father God I come to you now in the name of Jesus Christ your son, using the keys of binding & loosing things on earth. You gave them to Peter and he gave them to me.
My child is in bondage to _____
And I loose him in the mighty name of Jesus Christ! Satan turn him loose now and let him go! God said whatever I loose on earth, he will loose in the heavenly (demonic) realm and by faith, I am releasing him from your power, I abort your plans and destiny for his life. My child is going to turn to God and walk in the righteous steps he has planned for his life. God loves my child and Jesus Christ loves him and shed his blood for him that he might be saved from sin and its effects.
Father I thank you for the keys to the kingdom and I believe they will unlock the doors of bondage that are holding my child.
I thank you now Father God for working in that heavenly realm as I have worked in the earth realm.

To Loose Wives

Father God I come to you now in the name of Jesus Christ your son, using the keys of binding & loosing things on earth. You gave them to Peter and he gave them to me. My wife is in bondage to _____
And I loose her in the mighty name of Jesus Christ!
Satan turn her loose now and let her go! God said whatever I loose on earth, he will loose in the heavenly (demonic) realm and by faith I am releasing her from your power and I abort your plans and destiny for her life. My wife is going to turn to God and walk in the righteous steps he has planned for her. She will be a virtuous woman according to Prov. 31. God loves my wife and Jesus Christ loves her and shed his blood for her that she might be saved from sin and its bondages.
Father I thank you for the keys to the kingdom and I believe they

will unlock the doors of bondage that are holding my wife. I thank you now Father God for working in that heavenly realm as I have worked in the earth realm.

To Loose Husbands

Father God I come to you now in the name of Jesus Christ your son, using the keys of binding & loosing things on earth. You gave them to Peter and he gave them to me. My husband is in bondage to _____ And I loose him in the mighty name of Jesus Christ! Satan turn him loose now and let him go! God said whatever I loose on earth, he will loose in the heavenly (demonic) realm and by faith I am releasing him from your power, I abort your plans and destiny for his life. My husband is going to turn to God and walk in the righteous steps He has planned for his life. He will be the priest and head of our home. God loves my husband and Jesus Christ loves him, and shed his blood for him that he might be saved from sin and its effects.

Father I thank you for the keys to the kingdom and I believe they will unlock the doors of bondage that are holding my husband.

I thank you now Father God for loosing in that heavenly realm as I have loosed him in the earth realm.

Loosing Your Church

Father God I come to you now in the name of Jesus Christ your son, using the keys of binding & loosing things on earth. You gave them to Peter and he gave them to me. My church is in bondage to _____ And I loose it in the mighty name of Jesus Christ! Satan turn my church loose now and let it go! God said whatever I loose on earth, he will loose in the heavenly (demonic) realm and by faith I am releasing my church from your power, I abort your plans and destiny for my church. My church is going to turn to God and not walk in the traditions of men. The leaders are going free to obey the commandments God gave to his church. They will watch over the souls entrusted to them. They will have a true shepherds heart and will be servants to the flock. Our church is going to fulfill the great commission and be a lighthouse for God and many will come and accept Jesus Christ as their Lord and savior.

Father I thank you for the keys to the kingdom of God and I believe they will unlock the doors of bondage that are holding my church in darkness.

I thank you Father God for loosing in that heavenly realm as I have loosed in the earth realm.

Loosing Your Nation

Father God I come to you now in the name of Jesus Christ your son, using the keys of binding & loosing things on earth. You gave them to Peter and he gave them to me. My Nation is in bondage to _____ And I loose it in the mighty name of Jesus Christ!

Satan turn our Nation loose now and let it go! God said whatever I loose on earth, he will loose in the heavenly (demonic) realm and by faith I am releasing our nation from your power, I abort your plans and destiny for our nation. Our nation is going to turn to God and the people will walk in righteousness. The leaders are going free to obey God and his commandments. We will have God fearing Judges that will be fair and protect our constitution. Our nation is going to honor God and be a lighthouse for other nations to accept Jesus Christ as their Lord and savior.

Father I thank you for the keys to the kingdom of God and I believe they will unlock the doors of bondage that are holding our nation and its leaders in darkness. I believe righteousness will exalt our nation.

I thank you Father God for loosing in that heavenly realm as I have loosed in the earth realm.

Loosing from sickness, disease, & bondages

When I am ministering to a person in their presence, I like to lay hands on the person I am ministering to and say, "I loose you in Jesus name from this _____. God said whatever I loose on earth will be loosed in heaven and I loose this person from this _____.

Thank you Lord Jesus for taking stripes that we might be healed. You bore our sickness and carried our diseases, and by your stripes, we are healed.

You said signs would follow the believers so I thank you for the sign of healing in this person.

All Creation Is Waiting

*Romans 8:18-25 "For I consider that the sufferings of this present time are not worthy to be compared with the glory which shall be revealed in us. [19]For the earnest expectation of the creation eagerly waits for the revealing of the sons of God. [20]For the creation was subjected to futility, not willingly, but because of Him who subjected it in hope; [21]because the creation itself also will be delivered from the **bondage of corruption** into the glorious liberty of the children of God. [22]For we know that the whole creation groans and labors with birth pangs together until now. [23]Not only that, but we also who have the first fruits of the Spirit, even we ourselves groan within ourselves, eagerly waiting for the adoption, the redemption of our body. [24]For we were saved in this hope, but hope that is seen is not hope; for why does one still hope for what he sees? [25]But if we hope for what we do not see, we eagerly wait for it with perseverance."*

The curse that came through Adam and Eve is being reversed and the mature sons of God will be used to set all creation free. The sons and daughters of God will be using the keys of the kingdom to accomplish this!

Whatever you bind on earth will be bound in heaven and whatever you loose on earth will be loosed in heaven, by my Father which is in heaven!

Get Ready! Get ready! Deliverance is coming! Be wise and be purified! - Body, Soul, and Spirit 1st Thes 5:23 And the very God of peace sanctify you wholly; and I pray God your whole spirit and soul and body be preserved blameless unto

the coming of our Lord Jesus Christ.

Questions and Answers

Q - Is there a scripture that says a Christian can not have a demon?

A – No but there are many scriptures that say a Christian can have one. Jesus himself said deliverance is the children's bread. Not Satan's children ...but God's children!

Q - Can a Christian be possessed by demons?

A – The word possessed in the scriptures would be better translated to be demonized. Possession implies ownership and if we are born-again, our spirit belongs to God. Our flesh and soul (emotions) are dwelling places for spirits and various types of corruption and torment.

Q - What spirits could be in a Christian?

A - Spirits of Infirmities, Deaf spirit, dumb spirit, spirits of blindness, vexing spirits, spirits of heaviness, spirits of a broken heart, unclean spirits, spirits of grief. The word says that grief can consume your eyes, belly, and your soul. There are many other spirits that I will not list here.

Q – Can a person do self deliverance?

A – Scripture is silent on this but does not forbid it. I would not limit my deliverance to what I could cast out of myself. In ministering to yourself, renounce as evil, things that torment, oppress, or bind you. Also renounce all occult, cult, witchcraft, Ouija boards, horoscopes, palm reading, hypnosis, levitation, water witching, esp, tea leaf reading, abortion, séances, crystal balls, table tipping, dungeons & dragons, Harry Potter, all occult books, renounce all information you received from people in the occult, etc.

The list is endless! There are so many things out there in the world today to snare you! The new age and reincarnation are big snares! Follow Jesus Christ and get your wisdom and information from the word of God!

Q - Where do spirits go after being cast out of a person?

A – Spirits walk through dry places seeking rest. Spirits inside of a person are resting as they torment and oppress the person. They are doing their job and thus are fulfilled!

Q - Can a spirit be sent to hell or the abyss?

A – Jesus never did and did not instruct the church to do this.

Q – Can evil spirits dwell inside of animals?

A – Yes they went into the swine after Jesus cast them out of the Demoniac. My wife Betty and I were ministering deliverance to a group of people in our home years ago and a spirit of fear manifested in our poodle named angel. The fear entered her one day as she was chasing cars and a log truck almost ran over her. She gagged and whimpered as the spirit was leaving.

Q - How many spirits can be inside of a person?

A – At least a legion (a legion of Roman solders was 6,000). The spirit that spoke through the demoniac in Mark 5 said his name was legion. "For we are many."

Q – Can any believer cast out spirits or is that to be done by special ministries?

A – *In Mark 16:17 Jesus said "and these signs shall follow them that believe; In my name shall they cast out devils; they shall speak with new tongues; They shall take up serpents; and if they drink any deadly thing, it shall not hurt them; they shall lay hands on the sick, and they shall recover."*

Here Jesus said any believer could cast out spirits. Certain ministries in the 5 fold ministry will usually have special abilities (anointing), to be possibly more effective, so always be open and submissive to other ministries when you need help!
And He Himself gave some to be apostles, some prophets, some evangelists, and some pastors and teachers. (Eph 4:11)

Q - How do we try the spirits to see if they be of God or not?

A – The safe way to try the spirits is to listen to a person's message to see if in his message he confesses or declares that Jesus Christ is the son of God - born of a virgin, crucified on a cross, and raised bodily from the dead. The message should be pointing you toward Jesus Christ, who can forgive and save you from your sins. Be careful following signs and wonders being done by anyone who does not believe in the above!

Q – Can you cast spirits out of a person not being in the person's presence?

A – The woman of Canaan in Matt 15:21-28 had a daughter at home grievously tormented with a devil and Jesus set her free and he was not in her presence. The mother of the child was very persistent on getting Jesus to deliver her and would hardly take no for an answer.

We must earnestly desire help for ourselves and others. Jesus would always ask people if they wanted to be healed or delivered. He never forced himself on anyone.

How to Recognize Your Need for Deliverance

- ☐ Driving or obsessive, compulsive nature.
- ☐ Suicidal tendencies, withdrawal
- ☐ Bitterness, resentment, retaliation, rage, anger, vengence & violent nature.

☐ Heaviness, depression, stress, migraine headaches, pressure, confusion, irritability, hyper-activity. grief, heartache, sorrow, sadness.

☐ Mental illness, insanity, paranoia, manic depressive. hallucinations, fatigue, tiredness.

☐ Self mutilation, self hatred, low self-esteem self rejection, fear of rejection.

☐ Habits-addictions (drugs, alcohol, lust, pornography, masturbation, stealing, gossiping, excessive talking, food addict, excessive pleasure, various idols, blasphemy, filthy talking.)

☐ Fears & phobias (many fears and phobias).

☐ Infirmities, certain sicknesses & diseases
  & some deaf & dumb spirits.

☐ Schizophrenia, double mindedness

☐ Insomnia or excessive sleeping.

☐ Allergies (many).

  ☐ Vexed (disturbed, annoyed, tossed about).

☐ Occult spirits (from occult involvement).

☐ Witchcraft & sorcery spirits. Hypnosis, black & white magic.

☐ Unclean spirits (result of incest, homosexuality, lesbianism, effeminate behavior, adultery, fornication, bestiality.)

Do not use a band-aid for your problem but "be free indeed".

God Commands Us To Be Delivered!

" *[12]Therefore, my beloved, as you have always obeyed, not as in my presence only, but now much more in my absence, work out your own salvation with fear and trembling; [13]for it is God who* *works in you both to will and to do for His good pleasure." (Phil 2:12-13).*Here God is clearly working in you after being born-again, however He is continuing to work from the inside out.

Thayer's Lexicon gives as the primary meaning of this word salvation as "soteria". Thayer's Lexicon gives as the primary meaning of this word **"deliverance from the molestation of enemies". The enemies are the spirits and corruption in our soul and flesh that need to be cast out!** This is not an exhaustive list; however it gives a good overall understanding of when a person is demonized or under the influence of satanic oppression.

How God anointed Jesus of Nazareth with the Holy Ghost and with power; who went about doing good, and healing all that were oppressed of the devil; for God was with him.
God is with us and working through us by His Holy Spirit, therefore we can go about doing good and healing all that are oppressed of the devil!

HOW TO BE SAVED

The important thing in this life is to receive Jesus Christ as your Savior and Lord! Jesus said "I am the way, the truth, and the life: and no one cometh to the Father but by me. John 14:6

Say this prayer from your heart and Jesus will come into your life and your name will be written down in heaven.

Lord Jesus Christ, I believe you are the Son of God, born of a virgin, lived a sinless life, and became sin for me so I could confess and forsake my sins and be born of your spirit. I believe you were crucified on a cross and raised bodily from the dead. and have ascended into heaven where you are preparing a place for me. I am sorry for all the sins I have committed in the past and will turn from the old way of life I have been living. Come in to my life and save me from my sins. Thank you Lord Jesus for writing my name in heaven where I will live forever with you and all the other believers!

Now that you have been saved (justified) from your sins you should according to Heb 6 be baptized in water in obedience to God's command.

Your next goal should be to receive the Baptism of the

Holy Spirit. Read of this event in the book of Acts.

Acts 2:38-39 [38]Then Peter said to them, "Repent, and let every one of you be baptized in the name of Jesus Christ for the remission of sins; and you shall receive the gift of the Holy Spirit. [39]For the promise is to you and to your children, and to all who are afar off, as many as the Lord our God will call."

This experience will give you the power you need to witness and to be an overcomer.

TO ORDER ADDITIONAL COPIES OF THIS BOOK

THIS BOOK IS ALSO AVAILABLE ON CD READ BY THE AUTHOR

Contact:
Stan Johnson
P.O. Box 340
McLeansville, NC 27301

For Credit Card Orders
www.GladTidingsMinistry.org
Stan@GladTidingsMinistry.org